D1592937

BACH PERSPECTIVES

VOLUME 10

Bach and the Organ

BACH PERSPECTIVES

VOLUME 10

Bach and the Organ

Edited by
Matthew Dirst

UNIVERSITY OF ILLINOIS PRESS
URBANA, CHICAGO, AND SPRINGFIELD

Manufactured in the
United States of America
c 5 4 3 2 1
∞ This book is printed on acid-free paper.

Library of Congress Cataloging-in-Publication Data
Names: Dirst, Matthew.
Title: Bach and the organ / edited by Matthew Dirst.
Description: Urbana : University of Illinois Press, [2016] | Series: Bach perspectives ; volume 10 | Includes bibliographical references and index.
Identifiers: LCCN 2015041912 | ISBN 9780252040191 (cloth : alk. paper) | ISBN 9780252098413 (ebook)
Subjects: LCSH: Bach, Johann Sebastian, 1685–1750—Criticism and interpretation. | Organ—History—18th century.
Classification: LCC ML410.B13 B1515 2016 | DDC 786.5092—dc23
LC record available at http://lccn.loc.gov/2015041912

CONTENTS

PREFACE

Famously reproached in 1706 by the Arnstad consistory for his "curious" manner of playing chorales, the young Johann Sebastian Bach was already well on his way to becoming a "world-famous organist," according to the 1754 obituary authored jointly by C. P. E. Bach and Johann Friedrich Agricola. Sebastian Bach and the organ have been inseparable ever since. Renowned during his lifetime as a great player and as an expert judge of new instruments, Bach continues to set the bar for virtually all organists, who must master his music above all else. Considerable scholarly energy has also been devoted to Bach's compositions for the organ and his interaction with the organ culture of his time. This volume adds to that body of work with six essays exploring various aspects of Bach's organ-related activities.

In the first essay, Lynn Edwards Butler revisits a well-known primary source, Bach's 1717 report on Johann Scheibe's instrument for St. Paul's Church at Leipzig University, and sets straight a thoroughly checkered history. Scheibe emerges as something of a hero, not a hack, though one saddled with numerous challenges on this organ project in particular. Robin Leaver likewise focuses on a single problematic source, in this case a collection of Bach chorale harmonizations copied in Dresden sometime during the 1730s, and clarifies both its likely provenance and purpose. By situating this manuscript within a particular kind of pedagogy, Leaver enriches our understanding of Bach's routine teaching methods while providing a plausible scenario for its creation.

The remaining contributions concern themselves with two groups of organ works whose genesis and compositional history are still murky. Looking closely at various independent trio movements that Bach either composed or transcribed, likely during a crucial five-year period before composition of the better-known Six Sonatas for organ, George Stauffer proposes that these pieces served Bach in multiple ways: as a means of experimentation in the fashionable genre of the free trio and as pedagogical repertoire for advanced students. The other three essays, whose shared subject matter are church cantata movements with obbligato organ from Bach and a few key contemporaries, offer distinct conclusions plus a rich context for these works. Christoph Wolff and Gregory Butler both seek to uncover the "back history" of concerted Bach cantata movements that spotlight the organ, which have long been assumed to be transcriptions from earlier (lost) concertos. Their independent conclusions notwithstanding, both Wolff and Butler propose eminently plausible family trees of parent works and various compositional offspring. Matthew Cron, finally, provides a broad cultural frame for such pieces by noting how their various components engage in a larger discourse about the German Baroque organ: namely, its intimation of Heaven, which can be gleaned from a wide range of source material from Bach's day.

Earlier versions of four of these essays were presented at the conference "Bach and the Organ," sponsored jointly by the American Bach Society, the Eastman Rochester Organ Initiative, and the Westfield Center for Early Keyboard Studies and held at the Eastman School of Music in Rochester, New York, in September 2012; the others were solicited for this volume. I would like to thank the authors for their contributions, George Stauffer and Daniel Melamed for their work as general editors of Bach Perspectives (former and current, respectively), Christopher Holman for his bibliographic assistance, and Don Giller for setting the musical examples.

Matthew Dirst, editor

ABBREVIATIONS

BC — *Bach Compendium: Analytisch-bibliographisches Repertorium der Werke Johann Sebastian Bachs*. Edited by Hans-Joachim Schulze and Christoph Wolff. Leipzig: Peters, 1985–.

BDOK — *Bach Dokumente*. Edited by Andreas Glöckner, Anselm Hartinger, Karen Lehmann, Michael Maul, Werner Neumann, Hans-Joachim Schulze, Christoph Wolff. 7 vols. Kassel: Bärenreinter; Leipzig: VEB Deutscher Verlag für Musik, 1953–2008.

BWV — [Bach-Werke-Verzeichnis] *Thematisch-systematisches Verzeichnis der musikalischen Werke von Johann Sebastian Bach*. Revised edition. Edited by Wolfgang Schmieder. Wiesbaden: Breitkopf und Härtel, 1990.

KB — Kritischer Bericht (critical report) of the NBA.

NBA — [Neue Bach-Ausgabe] *Johann Sebastian Bach: Neue Ausgabe sämtlicher Werke*. Edited by Johann-Sebastian-Bach-Institut, Göttingen, and the Bach-Archiv, Leipzig. Kassel: Bärenreiter; Leipzig: Deutscher Verlag für Musik, 1954–2010.

NBR — *The New Bach Reader: A Life of Johann Sebastian Bach in Letters and Documents*. Edited by Hans T. David and Arthur Mendel. Revised and expanded by Christoph Wolff. New York: Norton, 1998.

OBH — *The Organs of J. S. Bach: A Handbook*. By Christoph Wolff and Markus Zepf. Translated by Lynn Edwards Butler. Urbana: University of Illinois Press, 2012.

SBB-PK — Staatsbibliothek zu Berlin, Preußischer Kulturbesitz, Musikabteilung, Berlin.

Bach's Report on Johann Scheibe's Organ for St. Paul's Church, Leipzig

A Reassessment

Lynn Edwards Butler

On Thursday, December 16, 1717, Johann Sebastian Bach, court Capellmeister in Cöthen, diligently examined the organ "partly newly built and partly renovated" by Johann Scheibe for St. Paul's Church at Leipzig University. At the examination, the university was represented by the then-current rector Carl Otto Rechenberg, former rector Johann Burkhard Mencke, and professors Johann Cyprian and Johann Wolfgang Trier.[1] Two days later Bach acknowledged receipt of twenty talers' compensation for testing the organ and for pointing out "the problems that might occasionally present themselves." His well-known written report, dated December 17, 1717, is preserved in the Leipzig University Archives.[2] Johann Kuhnau was cantor at the Thomas School and City Music Director at the time; Daniel Vetter, organist at St. Nicholas Church, had overseen the seven-year project.

Contemporary sources are unanimous in describing the examination as successful. Scheibe himself said the organ was "found [to be] free of even the smallest major defect,"[3] and the university agreed. Minutes of the administrative council at St. Paul's report that the examination revealed "no major defect . . . only a few inconsequential

1. Also in attendance, on behalf of Scheibe, were Lorentz Lieberoth, an organ builder from Mannsfeld, and Michael Steinert, organist at St. John Church in Leipzig.

2. Universitätsarchiv Leipzig (hereinafter UAL), Rep. II/III/B II 5, fols. 63r–64r (only the signature is autograph). See BDOK I, no. 87; NBR, no. 72; or OBH, 145–47.

3. "ohne dem geringsten Haupt Defect zu finden worden." Johann Scheibe, memorandum dated January 17, 1718, UAL, Rep. II/III/B II 5, fol. 77v.

items, as, for example, that the pipes were not yet properly tuned,[4] and also, that the space for the organ is somewhat too cramped, about which there was nothing the organ builder could do."[5] Vetter reported that there was "not one major defect" and, further, that Bach "could not praise and laud [the organ] enough, especially its rare stops."[6] According to Leipzig chronicler Christoph Ernst Sicul, Bach could "find little to complain of." The major parts of the organ had been "well made" and "nothing needed to be pointed out to the University." Anything that needed improvement either was fixed immediately or was excused.[7] Bach's nineteenth-century biographer Philipp Spitta viewed Bach's report as "highly favorable,"[8] and Bach scholar Arnold Schering considered Scheibe's organ "a masterpiece." "Scheibe's success, confirmed by no less a figure than Sebastian Bach," Schering wrote, demonstrated that the citizens of Leipzig "had not erred in their estimation of the local builder. . . . The University Church in Leipzig now owned one of the newest and most beautiful organs in Germany."[9]

While positive judgments continued for many years, a negative tone was set when Gottfried Silbermann's early twentieth-century biographer Ernst Flade—perhaps not the most objective voice as concerns Scheibe—claimed the university had received a decidedly mediocre instrument when Silbermann would have built a "masterpiece." Flade's views marked a turning point, and they seem to have influenced subsequent writers, who, without commenting on the positive aspects of Bach's report, instead

4. "Noch nicht reine ausgespielet" is the phrase used by the scribe. This translates directly as "not yet properly played in," which suggests the new organ needed time to settle in, in order to develop its true sound. The organ was tested more than a year after Scheibe had finished it, however, so this is unlikely to be the meaning. It is possible the scribe meant to write "noch nicht reine ausgestimmet," which can mean either "not yet properly tuned," "not yet tuned pure," or "not yet properly voiced." In light of Bach's report, any of these meanings makes sense.

5. "und wäre kein haupt *defect* an der Orgel zu befinden, sondern nur einige Kleinigkeiten, als zum *Exempel*, daß die Pfeiffen noch nicht reine ausgespielet wären, *it*: daß der Platz zur Orgel etwas zu enge sey, wo vor aber der Orgelmacher nicht könte." Council minutes dated January 28, 1718, UAL, Rep. I/XVI/I 13, fols. 460–61; cited in BDOK II, no. 88.

6. "ohne eintzigen Haupt-*defect* . . . daß er solches nicht gnugsam rühmen und loben können, sonderlich derer Raren Register." Daniel Vetter, memorandum dated January 28, 1718, UAL, II/III/B II 5, fol. 75r; cited in BDOK I, no. 87, and OBH, 46.

7. Christoph Ernst Sicul, *Anderen Beylage zu dem Leipziger Jahrbuche, aufs Jahre 1718* (Leipzig, 1718), 199. Cited in Carl Hermann Bitter, *Johann Sebastian Bach*, 2nd ed. (Berlin, 1881), 4:101, and in BDOK I, no. 87.

8. Philip Spitta, *Johann Sebastian Bach: His Work and Influence on the Music of Germany, 1685–1750*, translated by Clara Bell and John Alexander Fuller-Maitland (London, 1885), 2:9.

9. Arnold Schering, *Musikgeschichte Leipzigs*, vol. 2, *Von 1650 bis 1723* (Leipzig: Kistner and Siegel, 1926), 317.

emphasized what Flade labeled "Bach's serious concerns": the available space was used poorly, the wind was unsteady, the voicing uneven, the action heavy, and the wind chest design out-of-date.[10] Werner David called Bach's report "lukewarm and critical,"[11] a sentiment echoed by Hermann Busch, who concluded that because Bach had expressed reservations without giving any compliments, "the organ appears not to have impressed him very much."[12] In 1994 scholars became aware of the comments of Johann Andreas Silbermann, a nephew of Gottfried Silbermann's who visited the organ in 1741. According to him, "the tone and workmanship" of the twenty-five-year-old organ "did not accord with the report of Herr Capellmeister Bach."[13] The playing and stop actions were difficult, the Pedal reeds "not worth a damn," the internal layout confusing.[14] Silbermann's viewpoint seemed to confirm Flade's assessment, and this became the standard reading of the episode. In his recent study of repairs made to the organ after Scheibe's death, Andreas Glöckner thus emphasizes what he called the organ's "substantial construction problems."[15]

Fortunately, however, in assessing the success of the St. Paul's organ project we are not limited to the opinions of Scheibe's contemporaries, to the views of later writers, to sentiments ascribed to Bach, or even to Bach's report itself. Documents from the Leipzig University Archives, many of them written by Scheibe, make it possible to expand considerably on and to reassess the bird's-eye view that Bach's report gives us of the project and allow us to view it in a new context. They reveal the university's ambivalent and tight-fisted attitude toward the organ and its builder as well as Scheibe's

10. Ernst Flade, *Der Orgelbauer Gottfried Silbermann* (Leipzig: Kistner and Siegel, 1926), 50; and Ernst Flade, *Gottfried Silbermann: Ein Beitrag zur Geschichte des deutschen Orgel- und Klavierbaus im Zeitalter Bachs* (Leipzig: Breitkopf and Härtel, 1953), 93–94.

11. Werner David, *Johann Sebastian Bach's Orgeln* (Berlin: Berliner Musikinstrumenten-Sammlung, 1951), 45.

12. Hermann J. Busch, "Orgeln um Johann Sebastian Bach," in *Zur Interpretation der Orgelmusik Johann Sebastian Bachs*, edited by Ewald Kooiman, Gerhard Weinberger, and Hermann J. Busch (Berlin: Merseburger, 1995), 130.

13. Silbermann's knowledge of Bach's view of the organ came not from Bach's examination report but from reading and copying, "word for word," Sicul's report of Bach's examination.

14. See *Das Silbermann-Archiv: Der handschriftliche Nachlaß des Orgelmachers Johann Andreas Silbermann (1712–1783)*, edited by Marc Schaefer (Winterthur, Switzerland: Amadeus, 1994), 158. Also cited in BDOK V, 163.

15. Glöckner cites "uneven voicing, the relatively heavy action, and above all the continuously unstable wind pressure" (Schwankungen in der Intonation, die relativ schwergängige Traktur und vor allem den stets instabilen Winddruck). Andreas Glöckner, "Johann Sebastian Bach und die Universität Leipzig: Neue Quellen (Teil I)," *Bach-Jarhbuch* 94 (2008), 160–61.

heroic efforts to complete the project in a manner of which he could be proud. They allow us to understand more fully the problems enumerated in Bach's report, both those immediately fixable and those he believed likely to be encountered in the future, and they provide background for Bach's insistence that Scheibe be judged fairly and compensated fully.

In the first and fifth points of his report, Bach dealt with problems resulting from the "too tightly confined" case. Expectations regarding "roominess" changed in the eighteenth century. Andreas Werckmeister's well-known guide to testing an organ never explicitly mentions the need for a roomy case, although he does say that the key action "should not be too crowded," that pallets need to be easily accessible, and that problems may arise if pipes are mounted too close together.[16] In a later guide to testing, compiled by Jacob Adlung, a case so crowded that repairs were difficult to make was considered a major fault;[17] and in testing guidelines attributed to Gottfried Silbermann, one reads the same admonition.[18] At St. Paul's, Bach accepted Scheibe's explanation that he had not designed the case himself[19] and, further, that the university had refused his request for the additional space that would have allowed him to build more capaciously.

When it was decided in 1710 to dismantle the large organ and move it to the west gallery, it was agreed that a new case would be built for the organ, for which Scheibe provided an initial drawing. In his earliest estimate, dated September 6, 1710, Scheibe agreed to supervise the joiner and to instruct him how "one thing or another should be made according to my [Scheibe's] drawing and formulations."[20] The earliest preserved

16. *Werckmeister's Erweiterte und Verbesserte Orgelprobe [1698] in English*, translated by Gerhard Krapf (Raleigh, N.C.: Sunbury, 1976), 3, 9, 11.

17. "Ein Hauptfehler ist, wenn man die Orgeln allzuenge bauet" (it is a major fault to build organs too cramped). Jacob Adlung, *Musica mechanica organoedi*, edited posthumously by Johann Lorenz Albrecht with contributions by Johann Friedrich Agricola (Berlin: Birnstiel, 1768), § 347. Adlung's treatise on the art of organ building was written in the 1720s.

18. "When ample space is available in a gallery one should take care not to build things too close together; everything—such as the pallets, trackers, and the pipework—should be easy to reach. When an organ is too crowded and something quite minor occurs—as is often the case—and one cannot reach in or only with difficulty and at great pains, then often more harm is done than good. This would be a major fault." Cited in OBH, 150.

19. The term used by Bach, "verfertiget," means "drawn up" or "designed" and also "built." It is unlikely Scheibe meant he had not physically built the case himself—a disingenuous response at best—because organ builders rarely built the cases themselves but assigned the work to a joiner, to whom they supplied a drawing or design.

20. "wie dieses oder jenes nach meinem vorgeschriebenen Abriß und *formular* . . . soll gemachet werden." Johann Scheibe, memorandum dated September 6, 1710, *Specification derer Unkosten welche*

contract, an unsigned and undated draft, states that Scheibe would be responsible for "the entire organ—except the case, which will be made by the joiner."[21] But another case design may have been solicited as well, for "organ architect" Adam Orazio Casparini of Breslau was paid a modest fee for providing a case drawing *(Orgel-Riß)*.[22] As I suggested in a previous article,[23] the payment to Casparini raises the possibility that the organ's case was built according to Casparini's design rather than Scheibe's.[24] If so, it may have been when he was confronted with Casparini's design that Scheibe requested additional space so that he could "arrange the layout more capaciously." The university specifically required that the organ be placed in the gallery in such a way that as much sunlight as possible could enter through the west window, which restricted the size and shape of the case. As Bach reminded the university, Scheibe's

---

auff Seiten des Orgelmachers bey̆ Tranlocir- und reparirung der Pauliner Orgel aufflauffen möchten, UAL, Rep. I/XVI/I 15, fol. 66.

21. "in Summa die ganze Orgel /: ausgenommen was der Tischer an Gehäuse zu machen hat :/ in allen fertig liefern." Draft of contract, UAL, Rep. II/III/B II 5, fol. 30r.

22. "Einen *Species-Dukaten* vor H. Casparini, Orgelbauer in Breßlau zum *Gratial* wegen des überschickten Orgel-Rißes." UAL, Rep. II/III/B 1 5, fol. 224. Citing this payment made to Casparini, Burgemeister concluded that Casparini had provided the organ's disposition and made no comment about the façade design. Ludwig Burgemeister, *Der Orgelbau in Schlesien*, 2nd ed. (Frankfurt: Weidlich, 1973), 137.

23. See Lynn Edwards Butler and Gregory Butler, "'Rare, Newly Invented Stops': Scheibe's Organ for St. Paul's Church, Leipzig," in *Orphei Organi Antiqui: Essays in Honor of Harald Vogel*, edited by Cleveland Johnson (Seattle: Westfield Center for Early Keyboard Studies, 2006), 301–2, n21.

24. No matter what design was used, however, the case was already under construction when Gottfried Silbermann came to Leipzig in November 1710. In his absolute rejection of the university's plan to rebuild the organ, Silbermann warned that the proposed case would result in "unplayable" keyboards. Silbermann could have made his evaluation based on the construction itself (the joiner had started his work no later than November 1, 1710, and concluded on April 11, 1711), on a drawing by Casparini, or even on the drawing provided by Scheibe. Complicating matters even further, the case was, as we also know, altered during construction. The supplemental contract of May 26, 1715, required Scheibe to change a four-foot Principal into an eight-foot. Scheibe requested reimbursement for what he had had to pay the joiner for "building another case for the Brust[werk], not only because the previous one looked bad and ruined the façade, but also because it was not high enough, and the eight-foot pipes required by the contract would not have fit in otherwise" (vor Verfertigung eines andern Gehäuses zur Brust, weil das vorige nicht nur ein übles Ansehen gehabt, und den *Prospect* verderbet; sondern auch zu kurtz gewesen, und die in angezogenen *Contracte veraccordirte* 8. füßige Pfeiffen nicht raum darinne gehabt haben). Johann Scheibe, *Specification*, UAL, Rep. II/III/II B 5, fols. 68r–v. This raises the question of whether the engraving preserved in the Johann Andreas Silbermann diaries—the only representation of Scheibe's organ that has survived—was made before or after the organ case was constructed.

hands were tied; he had had to accommodate the internal layout to the restrictions of the allowable space as best he could.

In the report's second point, Bach confirmed that all essential parts of the organ had been "well and carefully built." There was nothing the university needed to be made aware of, except that there were occasional surges in the wind that needed to be minimized and that Scheibe had affixed the rollers to rollerboards, as was his practice, rather than mounting them on a frame. Vetter had described the old organ as "lacking strong wind," and he wanted the renovation to provide larger bellows valves and wind trunks with "adequate dimensions."[25] In fact, Scheibe built a completely new wind system at St. Paul's: new bellows, new wind trunks, new wind chests. Each of the six wedge bellows measured approximately eight feet by five feet and was equipped with counterweights;[26] the "6 new hair ropes," as they are referred to in Scheibe's receipt, cost 18 groschen.[27]

That the occasional wind surges were not considered a major fault is a point that needs emphasis, especially because Scheibe is often criticized for having built an organ with wind problems.[28] The schedule of subsequent bellows repairs, however, suggests normal wear and tear rather than any major defect. In addition, changing registration practices over time would have demanded ever stronger and steadier wind.[29] By

25. "da doch das alte Werck bey Versetzung auff den Chor einen guten Klang von sich geben wird, sonderlich, weil es ihm bishero an starckem Winde gefehlet, jetzo aber, denen Bälgen mit grossen *Ventilen* geholffen, künfftig auch die Wind Röhren mit gnugsamer Weite verbeßert werden sollen." Daniel Vetter, memorandum dated November 24, 1710, Rep. II/III/B II 6, fol. 9r.

26. As Johann Andreas Silbermann reported in 1741, "Herr Scheibe sagte mir, daß 6 Bälge an diesem Werck sind, jeder 4 Ehlen lang, 2¼ Ehle breyt, mit einer Falte." Schaefer, *Das Silbermann-Archiv*, 157.

27. Eighteen groschen were paid to organ builder Scheibe "vor 6. Neüe härene Stricke an die Bälge zu denen Gegengewichten." UAL, Rep. II/III/B I 5, fol. 245.

28. For example, Glöckner refers to the "substantial faults in construction" (erhebliche Konstruktionsmängel), especially the "continuously unstable wind pressure" (vor allem den stets instabilen Winddruck). Glöckner, "Bach und die Universität Leipzig," 160–61.

29. Bellows repairs were required only twice during the thirty years Scheibe took care of the organ: in 1718 and 1731, the first after a severe summer drought. In 1730, in a repair that was examined by J. S. Bach, Scheibe employed "an invention" to repair ciphering in the wind chest(s). Glöckner, "Bach und die Universität Leipzig," 165, citing council minutes dated September 28, 1730, UAL, Rep. I/XVI/I 34, fols. 133v–134r. Wind-system repairs were likely made during the twenty years (ca. 1750 to 1770) the organ was cared for by Johann Christian Immanuel Schweinefleisch, but no details are available. Nor do we know anything about Schweinefleisch's major repair in 1751 or the renovation in 1767. The bellows were replaced in 1774–75 by Schweinefleisch's successor, Johann Gottlieb Mauer; the wind chests were re-leathered around 1780 by Gottlob Göttlich; the "very worm-eaten" bellows were repaired by Christian Heinrich Wolf in 1790–92; and Johann Gottlob Trampeli built six new

comparison, it is worth noting that the large organ built by Christoph Contius for the Church of Our Lady in Halle is today considered a success, and Contius's reputation remains good, even though the wind pressure was too low for an organ of its size and the shaky wind in the Oberwerk was so severe that the examiners (including Bach) cited it as a major fault—that is, a fault that had to be corrected at the builder's expense before the organ could be accepted. Interestingly, the term used in Bach's Leipzig report—*stossen*, or surging, pushing—is unusual in passages concerning an organ's winding and is found in Werckmeister's treatise only in his discussion of the tuning problems that can occur when an organ has borrowed stops, or transmissions. Adlung was not against transmissions. He cited Werckmeister's passage in its entirety but added that problems could be avoided if a builder used the necessary intelligence and built with precision.[30]

Surprisingly, Bach's obvious preference for a frame rather than a rollerboard has rarely drawn attention from modern writers. Here Bach and Jacob Adlung seem to be in agreement. According to Adlung, it was sometimes "more convenient or satisfactory" to mount rollers in oak frames, a practice that had apparently become customary by the 1750s.[31] Werckmeister, by contrast, had decided against the practice. While a "strong oak frame" could provide a more dependable key alignment, he observed, it was nevertheless "best to retain conventional roller board construction" and to equip the keyboards with adjusting screws.[32]

---

bellows and replaced the wind trunks as part of a major renovation in 1802. See Veit Heller, "'Eine kleine Ehr'—Zum Status der Orgelbauer an der Universität Leipzig zwischen 1685 und 1850," in *600 Jahre Musik an der Universität Leipzig*, edited by Eszter Fontana (Leipzig: Stekovics, 2010), 125–26. In other words, the wind system regularly required repairs, and a major overhaul was necessary every twenty-five to thirty years. According to university organist Johann Gottfried Möller, Trampeli's work finally fixed "the extremely strong and to the instrument highly detrimental wind surges in the wind (nachtheilige Windstossen)." With all stops pulled, he reported, the instrument now had "reliably adequate, proper, and even wind, and thus also there is no more deficiency of wind (beÿ allen angezogenen Stimmen, beständig hinreichenden, richtigen und gleichen Wind hat, und also auch gar nicht mehr Windsiech [windsüchtig] ist)." Johann Gottfried Möller, memorandum dated October 21, 1802, UAL, Rep. II/III/B II 10, fol. 74r.

30. *Orgelprobe in English*, 33–34; Adlung, *Musica mechanica organoedi*, § 276.

31. "Anstatt des Wellenbretts bedienet man sich bisweilen mit großer Commodität eines eichenen Rahmens, an welchen man die Wellen bevestiget." Adlung, *Musica mechanica organoedi*, § 50. "Die Vorfahren befestigten die Wellen an dem Wellenbrete, an dessen Stelle bedient man sich ietzo eines Rahmens." Jacob Adlung, *Anleitung zur musikalischen Gelahrtheit* (Erfurt, 1758; Kassel: Bärenreiter, 1953), § 111.

32. "Some builders eliminate the roller board, mounting the rollers instead on a strong oaken frame; this seems to have the additional advantage of more permanent key alignment . . . others experiment

Bach's positive evaluation—the main parts of the organ had been "well and carefully built"—must have been very welcome to Scheibe. Early in the project Scheibe's skill had been disparaged by Vetter and cantor Johann Kuhnau, who told the university that the task of moving and repairing the large organ required no special ability and that they could recommend Scheibe as "honest, reasonable, and hardworking" (*redlich, billig, und fleißig*).[33] Some University Council members distrusted Scheibe's ability so much that they insisted on hearing the organ played in the midst of its repair and reconstruction, apparently while it was still dismantled. The newly repaired bellows, which were not fully dry, ripped apart during the demonstration, and new skins had to be procured.[34] The same council members then blamed Scheibe for the damage to the organ. These and other slights rankled. Seeking redress from the university, Scheibe wrote that his "honor and the possibility of being further recommended [had] suffered painful and irrevocable damage."[35]

In point three, Bach confirmed that Scheibe had provided the stops listed in the disposition as well as everything included in the contracts. Bach used the plural here: contracts. Contrary to what various writers have claimed—that proposals were received from Scheibe, Gottfried Silbermann, and Christoph Donat II, and that Scheibe's proposal was preferred by the university because he asked for less money and was a local builder besides—Scheibe did not compete for this job in the modern sense of this word. There is no rebuilding proposal from Scheibe, there is no proposal for a new organ, nor is there a disposition for a 3-manual, 54-stop organ associated with any of the contracts that have survived. Since none of the surviving contracts includes the organ's disposition, it is impossible to know exactly what Bach had in hand during the examination. Bach mentioned *two* Pedal reeds not built by Scheibe, but in a 1713 memorandum urging the project's completion, among the stops yet to be built Scheibe listed *four* reeds: Schallmey 4' and Cornett 2' in the Pedal, and Vox humana 8' and Schallmey 4' in the Hinterwerk. And in a memorandum written in 1716, Scheibe wrote that the university had "specifically prohibited" him from building *three* stops in case they would—as reeds do—"from time to time require either tuning or close

with a turned-around placement of the roller board . . . it is best to retain conventional roller board construction. If the [trackers to the] keyboards are equipped with adjusting screws, they can be constantly maintained in good regulation." *Orgelprobe in English*, 11.

33. Johann Kuhnau and Daniel Vetter, memorandum dated September 25, 1710, UAL, Rep. II/III/B II 6, fol. 3r.

34. Johann Scheibe, memorandum dated May 1, 1711, UAL, Rep. II/III/B/II/6, fol. 26r.

35. "alß ob ich das Werck angefangener maßen zu *perfectioniren* nicht *capable* wäre, dadurch meine Ehr und fernere *recommendation* empfindlichen und unwiederbringlichen Anstoß leiden müßen." Johann Scheibe, memorandum dated December 28, 1718, UAL, Rep. II/III/B II 5, fol. 86v.

attention,"[36] a circumstance Bach confirmed in his report. It is impossible to explain this discrepancy; however, it is easy to pick out the positions reserved for two Pedal reed stops in the engraving of the organ's stop knob arrangement.[37] On the right-hand side, in the second column in from the extreme right, among the Pedal stops are two stop knobs without names; one, below the Holl Flöten Bass 1', would have been for the Cornet 2'; the other, below the Trompet Bass 8', for the Schallmey 4'.

Bach also discussed the voicing, which had various faults that were to "be improved immediately." He specifically mentioned the lowest pipes of the Posaunenbass 16' and the Trompetenbass 8', which spoke "roughly" and with "a rattle," rather than with a pure and firm tone. These Pedal reeds had been newly built in the first phase of the project, the Posaunenbass with wooden rather than metal resonators. Vetter and Kuhnau envisioned a 16-foot stop with the same effect as the one Zacharias Thayssner had built for St. Nicholas Church, a stop imbued with gravity, strength, and, above all else, the ability "to penetrate . . . during congregational singing."[38] During the second phase of the project, when he was building the tin pipes for the façade, Scheibe was asked also to make the new Pedal reeds sweeter, or more elegant (*lieblich*). Again here, though, it is worth comparing the assessment in Leipzig with the assessment of Contius's organ in Halle, where the examiners requested additional voicing of the Subbass 16', the Posaunenbass 32', and of other reeds. It was not uncommon at examinations for builders to be asked to make improvements in voicing, especially of reeds.

At both St. Paul's and in Halle, it was noted that the organs would need to be tuned more accurately after the examinations. It was a sore point with Scheibe that the examination, which had been delayed for more than a year, then took place, as he put it, "in the worst possible weather."[39] Bach acknowledged this when he promised that

36. Scheibe's accounting included 200 talers "for 15 registers of new pipework built additionally in order to complete the instrument, because the instrument had been prepared for [18 registers] in the beginning, and an additional three registers belong there which had to be omitted because it was specifically prohibited to build any stops that would require tuning from time to time or strict attention" (Vor 15 Register neues Pfeiffwerck zur Vollständigkeit des Werckes annoch verfertiget; Maßen solches anfängl[ich] darzu angeleget ist, und noch 3. Register hinein gehören; welche aber deßwegen wegbleiben müßen, weil außdrücklich verbothen worden, keine Stim[m]en, die bißweilen gestimmet werden [emphasis in original], oder genauen Aufsicht darauf gehabt werden müßten, hinein zumachen). Johann Scheibe, memorandum dated October 29, 1716, UAL, Rep. II/III/B II 5, fol. 68r.

37. See BDOK IV, 128.

38. "Solches Stim Werck von so viel Schuh mit seiner *Gravität* und Stärcke über alle maßen durch dringen muß, wie an der Orgel zu St. Nicolai mitten unter dem Singen der Gemeine zu hören ist." UAL, Rep. II/III/B II 6, fol. 4r.

39. "und zwar bey den schlimmsten Wetter *examiniret*." UAL, Rep. II/III/B II 5, fol. 77v.

Scheibe would perfect the voicing and re-tune the organ when the "weather is better than it has been recently." Bach said nothing about either the pitch or the temperament, which suggests they were acceptable to him. Johann Adolph Scheibe, Scheibe's son and a music critic in Hamburg, wrote that the temperament at St. Paul's was "exceedingly comfortable and harmonious."[40] (In Halle, by contrast, after discussion at the examination, Contius agreed to reset the temperament.) The pitch at St. Paul's had been lowered at least a half tone, an item not included in the contract and also not billed separately by Scheibe, even though there was considerable work involved. Scheibe described the effort to bring the organ into "proper Chorton":

> In addition, not only were there many small matters taken care of for the instrument's better longevity, appearance and utility, but also it was brought into proper Chorton. This was requested by the musicians . . . and was also necessary so that the organ could be used with the usual instruments accompanying the church music.[41]

As already noted, Bach's report also dealt with some of the extra work Scheibe had done and included the recommendation that he be reimbursed for the parts newly built over the contract—in particular, "the new wind chest for the Brust." Flade erroneously thought Bach had found the Brustwerk chest so old-fashioned at the examination that he had insisted Scheibe build a new one and be paid a supplement for the additional work. In fact, Scheibe had already built two new wind chests for the Brustwerk; had he been required to rebuild them, this surely would have been considered a major fault in an instrument that suffered no major faults. The archival record suggests otherwise as well. Because the newly built organ was to have no Rückpositiv, the plan from the beginning had been to move the old Rückpositiv chest to "the Brust"—that is, into the interior, or breast, of the organ case. This new division, which became known as the Hinterwerk, was in addition to the already existing Brustwerk, which was retained and enlarged. When Bach talks about a new chest for "the Brust," then, he is referring to the new chest Scheibe built for the Hinterwerk "in the Brust." Long before Bach had written his report, Scheibe had already explained to the university why it had been necessary to build a new chest for the Hinterwerk rather than reusing the old

40. "die überaus bequeme und wohlklingende Temperatur." Johann Adolph Scheibe, *Der Critische Musicus, Erster Theil* (Hamburg: Thomas von Weiring's Heirs, 1738), unnumbered introduction. Previously cited in Lynn Edwards Butler, "Leipzig Organs in the Time of Bach," *Keyboard Perspectives 3*, edited by Annette Richards (2010), 90.

41. "über dieses Sind nicht alleine noch viel Kleinigkeiten, zu desto beßerer Dauer, Ziehrath und Nutzen des Werckes verfertiget, sondern es ist auch solches in richtigen Chor-Thon gebracht worden; Weil so wohl die zum Theil darzu verordneten als andere Musici, sehr darumb gebethen und verlanget; auch deßwegen nöthig gewesen, damit die bey Kirchen Music gewöhnlichen Instrumenta darzu gebrauchet werden können." Johann Scheibe, Specification, UAL, Rep. II/III/B II 5, fol. 69r.

Rückpositiv chest.[42] He gave the same reasons later cited by Bach: that a new chest had been necessary because the old chest had a table and only enough channels to accommodate a short-octave bass. It not only had been impossible to build a supplemental chest—perhaps because of the tightly confined case—but also would have been very time consuming and difficult to repair the old chest's warped table (one large piece of wood that covered the entire chest), a method of construction that in any event had gone out of favor. Bach noted one further reason why the new chest was necessary: it was important that all three keyboards have the same compass (with a "complete" rather than a "short" bottom octave), something that was neither necessary nor particularly desired in earlier organs but which clearly the Leipzig organists—and Bach—now considered essential.

At the examination Bach must have had a copy of Scheibe's bill in hand,[43] for Scheibe had specifically requested that his description of the extra work be available. One can be sure that if the university itself did not provide it to Bach, Scheibe would have. Other than the new wind chest, Bach made no mention of other items on Scheibe's list—such as the costs for building three new octaves of tin pipes for the Principal 8' in the Brustwerk and altering the façade so it would better accommodate it, for replacing the mouths in the old Principal 16' pipes remaining in the façade, or for building the cymbelstern and the pipes for the "cloudburst" at the top of the organ. Perhaps the university had already indicated its willingness to pay for these items, all of which relate to the organ's façade and appearance, but the record is clear that Rechenberg, the rector at the time of Bach's report, bargained stiffly with Scheibe, first inducing him to agree to 250 instead of 347 talers, and then forcing him to accept just 200 talers.[44] Bach also addressed, at Scheibe's request, the issue of amounts deducted from

42. In a memorandum written shortly before the organ's completion Scheibe referred to "a new chest in the Brust, because the old one that had been in the Rückpositiv, on account of its short octave, could not be used" (einer neuen Windlade in die Brust; weil die alte in den Rückpositiv gelegene, wegen der gehabten kurtzen *Octave* nicht gebraucht werden können) (*Specification*, UAL, Rep. II/III/B II 5, fol. 68r) and, in a memorandum written in 1717, before Bach's examination, to "the wind chest in the Brust, because the old one is no good, but still has a table" (die Windlade in der Brust, weil die alte nicht gut, sondern noch mit einen *Fundament*=bret) (Memorial, UAL, Rep. II/III/B II 5, fol. 70r).

43. Three slightly different versions exist of Scheibe's accounting of expenses over and above the contract. The earliest (Specification, UAL, Rep. II/III/B II 5, fols. 68r–69v) was submitted on October 29, 1716, shortly before Scheibe completed the organ in November; another version, undated (Memorial, UAL, Rep. II/III/B II 5, fols. 70r–72r), appears to have been written shortly before the organ's examination in 1717; and yet another version, also undated (UAL, Rep. II/III/B I 12, fol. 168r, cited in Glöckner, "Bach und die Universität Leipzig, 163), provided the basis for the settlement agreement arrived at on February 11, 1718.

44. The university claimed Scheibe owed rent, even though it had previously agreed Scheibe could live and work at St. Paul's without paying rent.

Scheibe's agreed-upon fee without his permission. The total was considerable—101 talers, according to one of Scheibe's calculations—for fees advanced to the sculptor, the painter, and Vetter, the project's overseer. Bach agreed it was not customary for such items to be charged to the organ builder and asked that Scheibe "not lose because of them." Here Bach's concern for Scheibe's financial welfare mirrored that of Johann Burkhard Mencke, who was rector during the important second phase of the organ's construction. Mencke urged the university to treat Scheibe fairly, noting that Scheibe, a dirt-poor man, had with certainty "not earned one taler of profit on the entire project, but likely had been forced into debt on account of it"—a project, he emphasized, "the equal of which is not often seen."[45]

Bach commented on two other issues: the unprotected window near the organ and the usual one-year guarantee offered by a builder. As already mentioned, the university was concerned that the organ not block light from the west window any more than necessary, and the earliest contract included this restriction among its provisions. A month before the joiner finished building the case, the university decided to improve the lighting by installing "larger, but still small" window panes,[46] and at the Easter fair in 1711, 720 *Doppelscheiben* and 720 *Spiegelscheiben* were purchased for the "window in the organ." Installing a window to the side of the organ was also considered. Scheibe agreed it was important that the organ have more light, but he complained in a memorandum written on May 1, 1711, that sawdust and tools dropped carelessly by the joiner had already been a great burden and annoyance during construction of the case. He was not sure how he could protect the organ from the damage certain to occur if the wall were broken into for a side window, but if it were going to happen, he recommended it be done before any more of the organ was set up.[47] The university's decision, taken shortly after receipt of Scheibe's memorandum, was to "make the organ window, and also the new window behind the pulpit,"[48] although it remains unclear whether "organ window" refers to a new window on the side or to installing the larger windowpanes in the existing window in the middle of the organ.

The summer before Bach came to examine it, the newly completed organ was severely damaged when windowpanes in the west window were shattered in a fierce

45. "daß er von diesem gantzen Bau, dergleichen doch nicht alle Jahre vorkommt, biß dato nicht einen Thlr. *Profit* hat; mag auch wol vielleicht noch darüber in einige Schulden gerathen seyn." Johann Burkhardt Mencke, memorandum dated November 22, 1716, UAL, Rep. II/III/B II 5, fol. 59r.

46. Council meeting of March 26, 1711, UAL, Rep. I/XVI/I 15, 282.

47. Johann Scheibe, memorandum dated May 1, 1711, UAL, Rep. II/III/B II 6, 26r; cited in Heller, "Eine kleine Ehr," 122–23.

48. "Solte das Fenster an der Orgel, wie das neue hinter der Cantzel, gemacht werden." Council minutes dated May 16, 1711, UAL, Rep. I/XVI/I 15, 359.

summer hailstorm and Scheibe had to repair damaged pipework. He urged the university to do whatever was necessary to protect the organ from inclement weather as well as summer heat, suggesting that the window behind the organ be bricked up at least as far as it was covered by the organ and did not allow any light into the church anyway—that is, about seven feet.[49] But even though the university agreed on September 28, 1717, to do this if it could be accomplished without inconveniencing the church or damaging the organ, nothing was done either before the organ's examination or after Bach had affirmed Scheibe's request by reiterating it in the examination report. Nor was action taken after Scheibe reminded the university the following January that it was necessary not only to fix the window but also to cover the back and top of the organ. Rather, the following spring it was decided simply to provide a window covering supported by mullions or a frame. We do not know how large the covering was or what it was made of, but in any event it did not stop sun from hitting the pipework. Johann Andreas Silbermann noted this in 1741, saying that because "the sun shone on part of the organ, this part was higher in pitch, and never in tune [with the rest]. Naturally."[50]

Finally, there is Bach's not-so-subtle point regarding the one-year warranty to consider. He reminded the university that it was normal practice for the builder to provide a guarantee for at least one year. Scheibe was willing to do this, he said, as long as "he is promptly and fully reimbursed for the costs he has incurred over-and-above the contract." In fact, the contracts signed by Scheibe on May 26 and December 5, 1715, both included a one-year warranty provision. Bach is basically saying, then, that Scheibe would be willing to meet the terms of his contracts *only if* the university "promptly and fully" reimbursed him for his out-of-pocket costs. It is a shameful chapter in the history of this project that the university paid neither promptly nor fully. Scheibe had first submitted his bill for expenses on October 29, 1716, along with his request that the organ be examined as soon as possible. Despite Bach's warning, Scheibe had still received no payment when he wrote again to the university on January 17, 1718. He repeated his request for payment of some 347 talers, reminding the university that at the examination the items built over the contract had been acknowledged as "indispensible."[51] In February 1718 the university forced Scheibe to accept only 200 talers, with 100 talers payable immediately and the remaining 100 talers due in September.

49. Johann Scheibe, *Memorial* (undated, but before November 24, 1717), UAL, Rep. II/III/B II 5, fol. 70v.

50. Schaefer, *Das Silbermann-Archiv*, 158. See also BDOK V, no. B485a.

51. "*specificier*eten Arbeit, welche, zu der verlangten Vollständigkeit des Werckes, nothwendich gemacht werden müßen, auch beÿ dem *Examine* vor unentbehrlich erkant worden sind." Johann Scheibe, memorandum dated January 17, 1718, UAL, Rep. II/III/B II 5, fol. 77r.

At the end of the year, when Scheibe still had not been paid in full, he threatened to satisfy his claim by, among other things, removing pipes from the organ. Finally, on March 19, 1720, almost three-and-a-half years after he had made his initial request, and fifteen months since Bach's examination, Scheibe received a final payment.[52]

The 200-taler settlement and the grudging payment of it are only two examples of the university's tight-fistedness and lack of support for the organ. The project was delayed for months and months, during which time Scheibe was not allowed to take on work elsewhere. When the project was finally resumed, it was only to build what was necessary to complete the façade; only under pressure from Johann Burkhard Mencke, who also served as counselor to the king in Dresden, did the university finally agree to use the balance of the funds in the organ bequest to build the remaining eighteen stops that had been prepared for from the beginning.[53] Mencke not only promised not to exceed the amount the university reluctantly agreed to—and if he did so, to pay the expenses himself—he also solicited private contributions from colleagues in both Leipzig and Dresden. The St. Paul's professors in charge wanted the project to be done with, but along the way Scheibe was often forced to suspend work because materials were not available. He and his family suffered hardship and loss in the unhealthy living quarters the university provided, and he even worked for a time without a contract in place because the university could not decide how to proceed. Scheibe was ordered by the university not to work at night; the keys to the church were taken from him. Against his will he was forced to sign a bond. Mistrusted by some of the professors, he apparently suffered slander in addition to financial loss.

In spite of this, Scheibe fought for recognition and fair treatment from the university, not only with respect to pay but also with respect to receiving the usual in-kind benefits, such as free housing during a major rebuilding project. Indeed, the need for patronage from the university may be one reason Scheibe felt forced, or was willing, to endure such unfavorable and unsupportive treatment. As Veit Heller recently observed, because organ builders were not members of a guild, the protection the university finally offered Scheibe when it made him an employee was very important,[54] shielding

52. Scheibe's struggle with the university over payment is described in Glöckner, "Bach und die Universität Leipzig," 161–64.

53. Resumption of the St. Paul's organ project in 1715 had been made possible by a generous gift from Gottlieb Gerhard Titius, professor of jurisprudence at the University of Leipzig, who died on April 10, 1714, and was buried in St. Paul's Church. Titius bequeathed 1,500 talers, expressing the wish that the money be used "to complete the organ" at St. Paul's. UAL, Rep. II/III/B I 11, fol. 1v. See also Sicul, *Leipziger Jahrbuche*, 261.

54. Scheibe was formally hired to maintain the organ on April 21, 1718. Council minutes dated April 21, 1718, UAL, Rep. I/XVI/I 13, 477–79. See also Glöckner, "Bach und die Universität Leipzig," 163.

him from attacks by competing artisans who were members of guilds and allowing him, for example, to take on apprentices.[55] As organ builder for the university, Scheibe enjoyed throughout his career the privileges the university's protection afforded.

In this context, then, Bach's examination report must be seen as a measured but forceful reproach of the university's actions. To repeat what I hope is now obvious: Bach's report enumerated the organ's immediately fixable problems as well as problems about which nothing could be done and problems likely to be encountered in the future. But the report is also a spirited defense of Scheibe: a document explaining why the organ builder should not be held responsible for anything he could not fix and why he should be paid, as he had requested more than a year before, for the work done over the contract. The record thus confirms reports that Bach's intervention on behalf of organ builders "went so far that, when he found the work really good and the sum agreed upon too small, so that the builder would evidently have been a loser by his work, he endeavored to induce those who had contracted for it to make a suitable addition—which he in fact obtained in several cases."[56] There is no doubt that Bach's reputation for doing all he could to ensure organ builders received fair remuneration was in part established here at St. Paul's in Leipzig. According to the builder (Scheibe), the buyer (the university), and the project's overseer (Vetter), Bach's examination revealed no major fault. Indeed, whereas Gottfried Silbermann's organs were criticized for "the all-too-uniform stoplists, which arise merely from an excessive caution in not risking stops of which he was not completely certain, so that nothing in them would miscarry for him,"[57] according to Vetter, Bach had not been able to "praise and laud [Scheibe's organ] enough, especially its rare stops, recently invented, and not to be found in very many places."

In spite of Bach's warning, and in spite of how poorly he was treated by the university, Scheibe never stopped caring for the organ he had "partly newly built and partly renovated." He repaired the organ after it was damaged in severe summer heat, he carried out a major cleaning of the organ twenty years after its completion, and he continued to live at St. Paul's and be paid to maintain the organ right up until his death in 1748.

55. Heller, "Eine kleine Ehr," 116–19.

56. Johann Nikolaus Forkel, *On Johann Sebastian Bach's Life, Genius, and Works*, in NBR, 441.

57. Johann Friedrich Agricola in Adlung, *Musica mechanica organoedi*, 212.

Bach's Choral-Buch?

The Significance of a Manuscript in the Sibley Library

Robin A. Leaver

In September 1936 the Sibley Library at the Eastman School of Music acquired a mid-eighteenth-century manuscript identified on its spine, in a contemporary hand, as "Sebastian Bach's Choral-Buch." It is a collection of chorales—melodies with figured bass, meant to accompany singing—given in a sequence similar to that found in many hymnals, beginning with the Sundays, festivals, and celebrations of the church year. This essay offers a description of that manuscript, a review of its provenance and content, and a discussion of its significance as a possible witness to the practices of the circle of organists who studied with Bach in the 1730s and 1740s.

DESCRIPTION AND PROVENANCE OF THE MANUSCRIPT

Spine (handwritten):	"Sebastian I Bach's I Choral- I Buch," mid-eighteenth-century hand.
Binding:	Mid-eighteenth-century half-bound vellum
Inside front cover:	Bookplate. "Sibley Musical Library Eastman School of Music"
Pencil: "KI G20"	
Title page:	"303614" [= Sibley accession number] *Sebast. Bach*, I 4 Stimmiges Choralbuch. [in a different hand from that of the spine and the main manuscript]
Pencil: Ms 489. Vault M 2138 B 118C	
Pages:	11 x 20.5 cm. Oblong
	* 9 unnumbered pages containing an alphabetical index of the first lines of the chorale settings, double columns per page, divided by double rule in red ink.
	* 3 unnumbered blank pages, divided by double rule in red ink.

* 1–285 numbered pages containing the chorales; each page usually ruled with six staves. (See table 1 for the detailed contents.)
* 18 unnumbered pages, some blank, some with inconsequential writing; most with ruled empty staves. There is evidence that at least one leaf has been removed from these pages at the end of the volume.
* It appears that the chorales were copied on separate sheets before trimming and binding, since some of the headings at the top of the pages have been cut, making them difficult to decipher.

According to library records, the manuscript was purchased from Hans P. Kraus, Vienna, in September 1936.[1] It had been listed as item number 70 in Kraus's second antiquarian catalog, with the following description:

> [Bach, Joh. Seb.,] Choralbuch. 238 Choralmelodien mit beziffertem Bass. Handschrift, die nach dem Schriftcharakter und der Orthographie zu schließen aus der Mitte des 18. Jahrhdts. stammt. Enthält auch Melodien, die von C. Ph. E. Bach nicht in das von ihm herausgegebene Choralbuch aufgenommen wurden. 286 S. Klein-Querquart. Hprgt. d. Zeit. Am Rücken zeitgenöss. Beschriftung: Seb. Bach's Choralbuch. Preis auf Anfrage.[2]

The title of Kraus's catalog suggests that the manuscript came from the library of the Prague musician and collector Joseph Proksch (1794–1864), which had been inherited by his great-nephew Robert Franz Proksch, who had died in 1933, a few years before Kraus issued his catalog. But what may have been true for other items in the Kraus catalog could not apply to this chorale manuscript because it was offered for sale around the same time by another Viennese antiquarian book dealer, Heinrich Hinterberger, and identified as part of the library of music theorist Heinrich Schenker (1867–1935). Kraus's catalog entry repeats almost verbatim that of Hintenberger's catalog (item No. 16),[3] confirming that the manuscript came from Schenker rather than Proksch:

1. "303614. Bach. Choralbuch. 4 Stimmides [sic]." 285 pages. 240 Sw. Francs. Gutter: 9/11/36 Kraus 240 Swiss Fr. *Condensed Accession Book: The Official Record of Each Volume Added to the Sibley Musical Library from Nov. 23, 1934 to April 6, 1937*, under the date: "September 10th 1936."

2. *Musikbibliothek Joseph Proksch Prag. Musikliteratur, Frühdrucke, Instrumental- und Vokalmusik, Erstausgabe: Antiquariatskatalog 2* (Vienna: Kraus, [1935]), 7. The Sibley Library owns a copy of this catalog.

3. Taken on its own, the Kraus catalog implies a different provenance to that given by Spitta (see herewith in main text) and opens the possibility that there were two similar manuscript collections of figured-bass chorales. But the Hinterberger catalog clearly establishes that there was only one such manuscript.

> Choralbuch. 238 Choralmelodien mit beziffertem Baß. Handschrift, die nach dem Schriftcharakter und der Orthographie zu schließen aus der Mitte des 18. Jahrhdts. stammt. Enthält auch Melodien, die von C. Ph. E. Bach nicht in das von ihm herausgegebene Choralbuch aufgenommen wurden. 286 SS. Klein-qu.-Quart. Hprgt. d. Zt. Am Rücken zeitgenöss. Beschriftung: Seb. Bach's Choralbuch. 250 [Swiss francs][4]

Before Schenker the manuscript was owned successively by Karl Konstantin Kraukling (1792–1873), royal librarian and museum director in Dresden, and then by his son and heir, the artist W. Kraukling. Sometime around 1880 the latter showed the manuscript to Philipp Spitta, who reported, "Herr W. Kraukling, of Dresden, possesses a chorale book with figured bass, in small quarto; on the pig-skin cover stands the words: 'Sebastian Bachs Choral-Buch.'"[5] A few years later a catalog of the manuscripts of Karl Kraukling was published in which the *Choralbuch* was listed among the few Bach items: "P[ièce] a[utograph] Sein [J. S. Bach's] 4stimmiges Choralbuch, eigenhändig geschrieben. 294 p. hpgb. [halbpergament gebunden] qu. 8." (An Autograph of his [Bach's] four-part Choralbuch, written in his own hand, 294 pages, half-bound in vellum).[6] That Spitta referred to the binding as pigskin, whereas the catalogs consistently (and correctly) describe it as half-bound in vellum, and that the number of pages differs in the sources (285 in one and 294 in the other), might suggest that there were two similar manuscripts. But there was only one such volume, and the variant page numbers can be explained by different approaches to counting the unnumbered leaves before and after the chorales. It remains a mystery why Spitta made the basic mistake of confusing vellum with pigskin; but perhaps this indicates that he only had a limited time in which to examine the manuscript. However, he was undoubtedly correct in stating that the handwriting of the figured bass chorales is not that of Bach, contradicting the view of the Krauklings. Spitta's conclusion is unequivocal: "The

4. *Katalog XII Musik und Theater: Enthaltend die Bibliothek des Herrn Dr. Heinrich Schenker, Wien* (Vienna: Hintenberger, [1935]), 4. That the Sibley Library paid Kraus 240 Swiss francs, and Hintenberger priced the manuscript at 250 Swiss francs in his catalog, suggests that the two Viennese antiquarian book dealers had some kind of business arrangement.

5. Philipp Spitta, *Johann Sebastian Bach* (Leipzig: Breitkopf and Härtel, 1873–1880; 4th ed., 1930), 2:589n2: "Herr W. Kraukling in Dresden besitzt ein Choralbuch mit bizziffertem Bass in klein Querquart; auf dem schweinsledernen Rücken steht: 'Sebastian Bachs Choral-Buch.'" Translation based on Philipp Spitta, *Johann Sebastian Bach, His Work and Influence on the Music of Germany, 1685–1750*, translated by Clara Bell and J. A. Fuller-Maitland (London: Novello, 1884–1885: reprint, New York: Dover, 1951), 3:108n149.

6. *Katalog der nachgelassenen Autograph-Sammlung des Königl: Bibliothekars und Direcktors des kgl. historischen Museums Herrn Constantin Kraukling in Dresden; Versteigerung zu Köln am 3. Dezember 1884* (Cologne: Heberle, 1884), 102, no. 3418.

volume exhibits, neither in Bach's handwriting nor in the composition of the chorales, a single trace of Bach's style or spirit."[7]

More recently Hans-Joachim Schulze identified the manuscript's current location in the Sibley Library but did not examine it in detail or offer an opinion substantially different from that of Spitta.[8] Schulze did suggest, however, that the handwriting on the spine of the *Choralbuch* is the same as that found in two other manuscripts copied by Carl August Thieme (1721–1795), a pupil of Bach's at the Thomasschule between 1735 and 1745.[9] Schulze thought that the heading of the *Pedal Exercitium* (BWV 598),[10] the title page of the 1738 figured-bass treatise together with corrections throughout the document,[11] and the handwritten title on the spine of the *Choralbuch* were all written by Thieme.[12] If so, then the manuscript *Choralbuch* would have strong Leipzig connections, suggesting an origin within the circle of Bach's pupils during the last fifteen years or so of his life. However, examination of facsimiles of the three documents gives rise to significant doubts as to whether they were indeed written by the same hand. There are certainly similarities but also significant differences among the handwriting of the three sources. Personal communication with Peter Wollny and Yoshitake Kobayashi established that the identification with Thieme cannot be supported.

Examination of the watermarks—none of which is complete because of the way the paper was cut to form the oblong format—reveals that the paper of the *Choralbuch* was made in the Bohemian paper mill in Dolní Poustevna (also known as Niedereinsiedel). The watermark in the center of the folio is of two capital letters in outline: "E S," within a circle crowned by a trefoil. Paper from this mill, with different forms of the watermark, was commonly used for musical manuscripts copied in Dresden in the 1740s and 1750s, according to the Saxon State and University Library Dresden

7. "'Sebastian Bachs Choralbuch': Das Büchlein zeigt aber weder Bachs Handschrift, noch auch im Satze der Choräle eine Spur Bachschen Stiles und Geistes." Spitta, *Johann Sebastian Bach, His Work and Influence*, 3:108n149.

8. Hans-Joachim Schulze, "'Sebastian Bachs Choral-Buch' in Rochester, NY?" *Bach-Jahrbuch* 67 (1981): 123–30.

9. Thieme studied subsequently at Leipzig University, was appointed Cantor of the Nikolaischule in 1752 and conrector of the Thomasschule from 1767. One of his predecessors in the latter position was Gottfried Vopelius (1645–1715), editor of the *Neu Leipziger Gesangbuch* (1682).

10. SBB-PK *Mus. ms. Bach P 491*; the notation is actually in the hand of C. P. E. Bach. See Hans-Joachim Schulze, *Studien zur Bach-Überlieferung im 18. Jahrhundert* (Leipzig: Peters, 1984), 126.

11. *J. S. Bach's Precepts and Principles for Playing the Thorough-Bass or Accompanying in Four Parts, Leipzig 1738*, translated and edited by Pamela L. Poulin (Oxford: Clarendon, 1994), xiii, 60.

12. Schulze, "Sebastian Bachs Choral-Buch," 129–30.

(SLUB).[13] Mary Oleskiewicz, who has conducted independent research into Dresden manuscripts, informs me in correspondence that this particular variant of the watermark is similar to that found in a significant number of Dresden sources (with music by Quantz, Telemann, and others) that date from before 1740. From this it would appear that the Sibley *Choralbuch* originated in Dresden sometime between 1730 and 1740. The list of potential original owners includes no less than three Dresden organists who had studied with Bach in Leipzig: his eldest son Wilhelm Friedemann, Gottfried August Homilius, and Christian Heinrich Gräbner.

Bach and His Dresden Connections

Bach continued to maintain contacts with the Dresden court musicians throughout the 1730s and 1740s. In his "Short but Most Necessary Draft for a Well-Appointed Church Music," presented to the Leipzig town council in 1730, he makes reference to the virtuosi of the Dresden court, whom he clearly knew.[14] In 1733 he applied for court recognition by sending his *Missa* (BWV 232/1) to Dresden. On receiving the title of "Electoral Saxon and Royal Polish Court Composer" in 1736,[15] he gave a two-hour recital on December 1 on the new Silbermann organ of the Frauenkirche, in the presence of the Russian ambassador, Baron von Keyserlingk, "and many Persons of Rank, also a large attendance of other persons and artists." The account also records that Bach was heard "with particular admiration."[16]

The first of Bach's pupils to serve a Dresden church as organist during the time in question was Wilhelm Friedemann Bach, who on the death of Christian Petzold in 1733 became the organist of the Sophienkirche, a position he held until 1746. This was a particularly important position since the Sophienkirche also functioned at that time as the Lutheran Saxon court chapel,[17] which paralleled the Catholic court chapel

13. *Musik der Dresdner Hofkapelle: Schrank II; Die Instrumentalmusik zur Zeit der sächsisch-polnischen Union; Wasserzeichenkataloge*. Available at http://www.schrank-zwei.de/recherche/schreiber-wasserzeichenkataloge, W-Dl-025, 045–051, 053–061: manuscript scores and parts of music by Franz Benda, Johann Friedrich Fasch, Christian Petzold, Johann Joachim Quantz, Georg Philipp Telemann, among others.

14. BDOK I, 63 (no. 22); NBR, 150 (no. 151).

15. Bach's name as "Hof-Compositeur" appears for the first time in the *Sächsischer Hoff- und Staats Calender* in 1738.

16. BDOK II, 279 (no. 389); NBR, 188 (no. 191).

17. "Die Kirche zu St. Sophien, worinnen auch der Evangelische Hof-Gottesdienst gehalten wird." *Des grossen Zebaoths höchst-wohlgefällige Gottesdiensts-Ordnung in dem Evangelischen Zion der Kön. Pohln. und Churfürstl. Sächß. Residentz Dreßden* (Dresden: Mohrenthale, 1745), sig. 2r. This arrangement began in 1737; see Reinhard Vollhardt, *Geschichte der Cantoren und Organisten von den Städten im Königreich Sachsen: Ergänungen und Berichtigungen von Eberhard Stimmel* (Leipzig: Peters, 1978), 86.

within the electoral residence. Unfortunately, no *Choralbuch* connected with Wilhelm Friedemann is known, and the seven chorale preludes attributed to him are undoubtedly spurious.[18] A renowned improviser, he evidently had no need of such written "aides-mémoire" for chorale preludes and chorale accompaniments.

Gottfried August Homilius, who began his studies with Bach in Leipzig in 1735, was appointed organist of the newly built Frauenkirche in Dresden in 1742. In 1755 he became the *Kreuzkantor* and *director musices* for Dresden's three main churches.[19] During his early years as organist of the Frauenkirche, he most likely compiled his manuscript *Choralbuch* of 198 melodies with figured bass, a collection now in private hands.[20]

Christian Heinrich Gräbner, finally, came from a distinguished family of Dresden organ builders and organists that included his grandfather, father, two uncles, brother, and nephew.[21] His father, Johann Heinrich Gräbner, at various times organist of both the Frauenkirche and Sophienkirche,[22] consolidated his connection to the Dresden court at the beginning of the eighteenth century by becoming "Hof-Orgelmacher," a position that also involved making harpsichords.[23] It seems highly likely that Johann Heinrich Gräbner heard Bach perform in Dresden in 1717 following the Louis Marchand episode[24] and perhaps also on other unrecorded occasions. In 1725—the year Bach "performed for over an hour on the new organ of the Sophienkirche"[25]—Johann Heinrich Gräbner sent his son Christian Heinrich to study with Bach in Leipzig for

18. See David Schulenberg, *The Music of Wilhelm Friedemann Bach* (Rochester, N.Y.: University of Rochester Press, 2010), 66–67.

19. Uwe Wolf, *Gottfried August Homilius: Studien zu Leben und Werk* (Stuttgart: Carus, 2009), 11.

20. Wolf, *Gottfried August Homilius*, 90–92. A smaller ms. collection was later created totaling 148 melodies: 115 from the first collection with 33 additional melodies; see Wolf, *Gottfried August Homilius*, 34–35, 92. Two other manuscript organ chorale collections of Homilius, comprising 220 and 303 chorales, respectively, were in the Königlichen Bibliothek, Dresden, until they were destroyed during World War II (see Robert Eitner, *Biographisch-Bibliographisches Quellen-Lexikon der Musiker und Musikgelehrten* [Leipzig: Breitkopf and Härtel, 1900–1903], 5:198). Homilius later created a ms. collection of 197 four-part chorales, dated 1780 (Wolf, *Gottfried August Homilius*, 88–90).

21. See Ulrich Dähnert, *Historische Orgeln in Sachsen: Ein Orgelinventar* (Leipzig: VEB Deutscher Verlag für Musik, 1983), 303 and variously.

22. See Vollhardt, *Geschichte der Cantoren und Organisten*, 76, 86.

23. See, for example, *Königl. Polnischer und Churfürstl. Sächsischer Hoff- und Staats Calender Auf das Jahre 1728* (Leipzig: Weidmann, 1728), sig. a3r. J. H. Gräbner had held the position since 1702: see Janice B. Stockigt, "The Court of Saxony-Dresden," *Music at German Courts, 1715–1760: Changing Artistic Priorities*, edited by Samatha Owens, Barbara M. Ruel, and Janice B. Stockogt (Woodbridge, Suffolk: Boydell, 2011), 39.

24. See BDOK II, 348 (no. 441) and 3:83–84 (no. 666); NBR, 79–80, 301 (nos. 67 and 306).

25. NBR, 117 (no. 118); BDOK II: 150 (no. 193).

the next two years, at "no small cost" to himself.[26] Around 1727 Christian Heinrich Gräbner returned to Dresden, where he substituted for his father on the organ of the Frauenkirche and also played services at the Sophienkirche until 1733, when Wilhelm Friedemann Bach became organist of that church. On Johann Heinrich Gräbner's death in 1739, Christian Heinrich Gräbner succeeded his father as the organist of the Frauenkirche; three years later he became the organist of the Kreuzkirche, and Homilius replaced him at the Frauenkirche. Gräbner remained at the Kreuzkirche for the rest of his life.[27] During his last fourteen years (1755–1769) he worked closely with Homilius, who was then Kreutzkantor. Connections between the Gräbners and the Dresden court continued, with Christian Heinrich's brother Johann Heinrich [Jr.] taking over the responsibilities for harpsichord making from their father in 1735[28] and on their father's death in 1739 succeeding him as "Hof-Orgelmacher."

Characteristics of the Sibley *Choralbuch*

This anthology was clearly compiled primarily for practical purposes. To begin with, the melodies follow the sequence found in many Lutheran hymnals, beginning with church-year hymns—Advent, Christmas, Epiphany, Passion, Easter, Ascension, Pentecost, Trinity, saints days—and continuing with such sections as catechism, Christian life, funeral hymns, last judgment, heaven and hell, and eternal life (the melodies, in the sequence of the *Choralbuch*, are listed in table 1). The practical nature of the anthology is evident in the frequent "aides-mémoire" for the organist, which remind the player of the number of stanzas to be sung by including both the number of the last stanza together with its textual incipit.

According to Johannes Zahn,[29] the earliest source for two of the melodies found in the Sibley *Choralbuch*—*Mein Jesu dem die Seraphinen* (Zahn 5991) and *Warum solt ich mich denn grämen* (Zahn 6468)—dates from after Bach's death. This source is an untitled manuscript *Choralbuch*, which Zahn found in the Saxon Royal Library, Dresden, blind-

26. BDOK II, 228 (no. 319): "welches mich nicht wenig gekostet." Johann Heinrich Gräbner recorded this on October 4, 1732; see also his similar statement made some five years earlier, under the date of November 4, 1727: BDOK, II, 178 (no. 238). During Christian Heinrich Gräbner's time in Leipzig, the organist of the Thomaskirche was Christian Gräbner (appointed in 1701; died in 1729), who may or may not have been a relative; see Arnold Schering, *Johann Sebastian Bach und das Musiklebens Leipzigs im 18. Jahrhundert* [Der Musikgeschichte Leipzigs dritter Band von 1723 bis 1800] (Leipzig: Kistner and Siegel, 1942; reprint, Leipzig: Zentralantiquariat, 1974), 62.

27. Vollhardt, *Geschichte der Cantoren und Organisten*, 74, 76.

28. Edward L. Kottick, *A History of the Harpsichord* (Bloomington: Indiana University Press, 2003), 331, 511n111.

29. Johannes Zahn, *Die Melodien der deutschen evangelischen Kirchenlieder* (Gütersloh: Bertelsmann, 1889–1893; reprint, Hildesheim: Olms, 1963).

stamped on the cover with the year "1752." Zahn reports that its index corresponds to the content of the 1724 Dresden *Gesang-Buch*, which was reprinted numerous times in both Dresden and Leipzig.[30] The Dresden *Gesang-Buch* was widely used in Leipzig: in 1732, just two years before the official Leipzig *Gesangbuch* was published, a handwritten note from Johann Matthias Gesner, rector of the Thomasschule, indicated that every Thomaner should have his own copy of the Dresden *Gesang-Buch*.[31] *Das privilegirte Vollständige und vermehrte Leipziger Gesangbuch*, first published in 1734, included an index that identifies where its hymn-texts could also be found in the Dresden *Gesang-Buch*.[32] Thus the 1752 Dresden manuscript *Choralbuch* examined by Zahn reflects both Leipzig and Dresden usage. Zahn also notes that this collection contains mostly older melodies but is marred by many errors committed by the copyist, who was not a well-trained musician.[33]

Though Zahn's anthology is comprehensive with regard to printed sources, it is somewhat cursory with regard to manuscript sources, being limited to *Choralbücher* in Zahn's possession and those he found in the libraries he visited: only twenty Lutheran manuscript chorale collections dating between 1700 and 1750 but not the Sibley Library *Choralbuch*.[34] As yet there is no bibliographical control for such sources, which are numerous in libraries around the world and in private hands; previously unrecorded manuscripts keep coming to light as well. Thus Zahn's information regarding these two tunes means only that the Dresden *Choralbuch* of 1752 was the earliest source that he was able to locate. The Sibley *Choralbuch*, which appears to date from the previous decade, or even earlier, is therefore (thus far) the earliest known source for these melodies. It is also competently scribed and would seem to be a more reliable source than the 1752 Dresden manuscript that Zahn examined.

There are contemporary references to manuscript *Choralbücher*, and a few of them are connected to Bach. In his New Year catalog of 1764, Breitkopf offered for sale two

30. See Werner Neuman, "Zu frage der Gesangbücher Johann Sebastian Bachs," *Bach-Jahrbuch* 43 (1956): 115n9.

31. Neuman, "Zur frage der Gesangbücher," 114. A copy of the first edition of Dresden *Gesangbuch* of 1724 must have been accessible in the Bach household soon after its publication. A setting of *Schaffs mit mir Gott*, a text that made its first appearance in the 1724 hymnal, with music probably composed by Bach (BWV 514), was copied by Anna Magdalena into her *Notenbuch* begun in 1725.

32. The index was included in later reprints.

33. "Es ist fehlerhaft geschrieben . . . Der Schreiber war kein gut geschulter Musiker" (Zahn, *Die Melodien*, 6:543).

34. See Zahn, *Die Melodien*, 6:535–41. To date there has been no systematic and comprehensive attempt to locate eighteenth-century manuscript *Choralbücher* with a view toward creating a bibliographic database of sources, compiling an anthology of chorale melodies, and establishing their variant forms.

different manuscript collections of chorales harmonized by Bach. The first is listed (on page 7) as "Bach, J. S. Capelmeisters und Musikdirectors in Leipzig, 150 Choräle, mit 4 Stimmen. *a* 6 thl.[150 Chorales in 4 parts]," while the second (page 29) advertizes "Bachs, J. S. Vollständiges Choralbuch mit Noten aufgesetzten Generalbasse an 240 in Leipzig gewöhnlichen Melodien. 10 thl." [Complete Choral Book with notes set with figured bass comprising 240 melodies in use in Leipzig].[35] The first title has been identified as the chorales collected by Bach's pupil Johann Ludwig Dietel sometime around 1735.[36] The second manuscript has been dismissed as being an otherwise unknown and lost source: Spitta simply states that "this important collection is lost," and others have followed his lead.[37]

But the latter entry in Breitkopf's 1764 catalog reads like a fairly accurate description of the Sibley *Choralbuch*: indeed, its four descriptive features are a perfect match. First, it is a complete (Vollständiges) *Choralbuch*, meaning that it is not a random collection of chorales but a comprehensive anthology required for congregational use throughout the church year on various liturgical occasions, and it is structured accordingly. Second, the melodies are set with figured bass rather than being fully realized in four parts. Third, the Breitkopf catalog records that the *Choralbuch* comprises 240 melodies, and the booksellers' catalogs of the mid-1930s state that the Sibley manuscript contains 238.[38] Fourth, the Breitkopf catalog links the repertoire with Leipzig use, and, as reported above, there was much common hymnody between the Leipzig and Dresden churches.

35. BDOK III, 165–66 (no. 711).

36. Musikbibliothek der Stadt Leipzig, Ms. R 18; NBA III/2.1, 21–26. See also Peter Krause, *Handschriften der Werke Johann Sebastian Bachs in der Musikbibliothek der Stadt Leipzig* (Leipzig: Musikbibliothek, 1964), 51–52; Hans-Joachim Schulze, "'150 Stück von den Bachischen Erben': Zur Überlieferung der vierstimmigen Choräle Johann Sebastian Bachs," *Bach-Jahrbuch* 69 (1983): 81–100.

37. Spitta, *Johann Sebastian Bach*, 2:589: "Dieses wichtige Sammelwerk ist verloren gegangen"; Spitta, *Johann Sebastian Bach, His Work and Influence*, 3:108. See also Schulze, "Sebastian Bachs Choral-Buch," 130; NBA KB III/2.2, 82.

38. The Dietel chorale collection is described in the Breitkopf catalog as comprising 150 chorales, whereas the actual number is 149. The total of 238 for the Sibley *Choralbuch* is the number given in the Viennese catalogs of the mid-1930s and is clearly an approximation, depending on whether alternative harmonizations assigned to different texts and alternative harmonizations of a melody associated with a single text are counted. For example, there are four different harmonizations of *Wir glauben all an einen Gott* in the Sibley *Choralbuch*. Are variants to be counted as different tunes? Should *Kyrie, Gott Vater in Ewigkeit* be considered as one tune or three, one for each stanza? If one simply counts the number of different harmonizations, then the total is actually 226, but four of these are duplicates: the copyist lost his place and repeated them. There are at least 173 different melodies, some of which are set multiple times.

Chorale Harmonizations and Bach's Pedagogy

Two strands of chorale harmonization are closely associated with Lutheran organists and their pupils. On the one hand, there are the four-part settings from the vocal works that have been the foundation for teaching harmony since their initial publication in the late eighteenth century. On the other are harmonizations used to accompany congregational singing. Jacob Adlung, who had studied with Bach's second cousin Johann Nikolaus Bach in Jena, notes the inherent variety in the latter category in his 1758 *Anleitung zu den musikalischen Gelahrtheit*. Organists, he notes, must master four skills: realizing figured bass, the "science" (*Wissenschaft*) of accompanying chorales, playing from tablature, and improvisation.[39]

The science of accompanying chorales was to a large extent a hidden tradition because organists generally improvised accompaniments to congregational song. But in Bach's case, his pupils preserved a few examples of chorale accompaniments from the master's hand. These chorale settings are rarely heard because they are not preludes to be played before the singing of a hymn but rather hymn accompaniments—some of them complete with *Zwischenspiele*, interludes in between each melodic line. Perhaps the most familiar of these is *In dulci jubilo*, BWV 729 (heard annually on Christmas Eve, at the end of the King's College, Cambridge, Service of Lessons and Carols). The oldest source of this setting is found in a collection of organ music among entries in the hand of Johann Tobias Krebs the Elder, who studied with Bach in Weimar between 1714 and 1717. This version (BWV 729a) is not fully written out in four parts but comprises just melody and bass with the harmony designated by figures[40] and is one of four chorale settings by Bach in Krebs's manuscript:

Gelobet seist du, Jesus Christ (BWV 722a)
Vom Himmel hoch (BWV 738a)
In dulci jubilo (BWV 729a)
Lobt Gott, ihr Christen, allzugleich (BWV 732a)

The fact that all of these harmonizations of Christmas chorale melodies are in Krebs's hand confirms that Bach was careful to instruct at least this pupil in the art (or "science," according to Adlung) of accompanying congregational singing.

39. Jacob Adlung, *Anleitung zu den musikalischen Gelahrtheit* (Erfurt: Jungnicol, 1758), 625 (§ 300). Johann Ernst Bach, who studied with his uncle J. S. Bach in Leipzig between 1737 and 1742 and was subsequently Hofkapellmeister in Eisenach, wrote the preface. The first chapter of Daniel Gottlob Türk's *Von den wichtigsten Pflichten eines Organisten* (Halle: Türk, 1787; reprint, Hilversum: Knuf, 1966) also deals with chorale accompaniment: see Daniel Gottlob Türk, *On the Role of the Organist in Worship*, translated by Margot Ann Greenlimb Woolard (Lanham, Md.: Scarecrow, 2000).

40. SBB-PK *Mus. ms. Bach P 802*.

There are other similar examples preserved somewhat later by Johann Peter Kellner. An organist and teacher who was particularly active in Leipzig in the mid-1720s, Kellner was possibly a student of Bach and certainly an avid collector of his works.[41] Like the examples recorded by Krebs the Elder, the chorale settings preserved by Kellner are congregational accompaniments rather than preludes to such singing, though now fully written out instead of melodies with figured bass. The Kellner group includes *Allein Gott in der Höh sei Ehr* (BWV 715) and *Herr Jesu Christ dich zu uns wend* (BWV 726), melodies that were sung virtually every week in Lutheran worship.[42] There is also Bach's harmonization in the same restrained style for Luther's German Te Deum, *Herr Gott dich loben wir* (BWV 725), which turned up somewhat late in the eighteenth century.

On such chorale accompaniments, Spitta comments as follows:

> Pupils of Bach who took down copies of his organ chorales [chorale preludes] appended to them the two-part figured settings from Bach's chorale book, when they could get access to them. Thus when they played the organ prelude, they could afterwards use the melody, as harmonised by their revered master, for accompanying the congregational singing. . . . The interludes introduced in them show that they were written for the very purpose of accompanying the congregation. The harmonising, which is of rare originality and power, makes us feel how much we have to regret in the loss of the whole chorale book.[43]

Spitta seems to have written these words before seeing the manuscript *Choralbuch* in Dresden. Though a Bach *Choralbuch* with harmonizations for congregational singing was not extant, Spitta was certain that such a collection had once existed.[44] He did not consider the *Choralbuch* he saw in Dresden, which now lives in the Sibley Library, to be this lost anthology of harmonizations by Bach because none of the settings seemed daring enough to have confused the Arnstadt congregation with "many strange tones."[45] Nor did these settings resemble those recorded by Krebs the Elder in Weimar, with their *Zwischenspiele*, or the report of Bach's imaginative improvisation on the hymn *Wir glauben all an einen Gott* on the Trost organ in Altenburg in 1739. On the latter occasion an anonymous witness reported:

41. On Kellner, see Russell Stinson, *The Bach Manuscripts of Johann Peter Kellner and His Circle: A Case Study in Reception History* (Durham, N.C.: Duke University Press, 1989), 13–19.

42. Both are found in SBB-PK *Mus. ms. Bach P 804*, fascicle 42.

43. Spitta, *Johann Sebastian Bach*, 2:589; Spitta, *Johann Sebastian Bach, His Work and Influence*, 3:108–9.

44. See note 7.

45. BDOK II, no. 16; NBR, no. 20.

> Few are in a position to guide a congregation as old Bach could do, who one time on the large organ in Altenburg played the creedal hymn in D minor, but raised the congregation to E-flat minor for the second verse, and on the third verse even went to E minor. Only a Bach could do this and only the organ in Altenburg. Not all of us are or have that.[46]

What Spitta apparently did not consider was that in his particular pedagogical system, Bach required basic skills in harmonization before pupils were allowed to emulate his own improvised chorale accompaniments. In order to do this, he seems to have compiled a collection of chorales in which the harmonizations are restrained and the harmonic rhythm is slow.

Various documents, notably prefaces to printed *Choralbücher*, say explicitly that accompanying congregational singing is an art demanding sensitivity, thus extreme flights of harmonic fancy are to be avoided. For example, a contract (dated December 14, 1713) that offered to Bach the position as organist of the Marktkirche in Halle as Zachow's successor, includes the following detailed provision:

> He is obliged . . . to take care to accompany attentively the regular chorales and those prescribed by the Minister, before and after the Sermons on Sundays and feast days, as well as Communion and at Vespers and on eves of holidays, slowly and without unusual embellishment, in four or five parts, on the Diapason, to change the other stops at each verse, also to use the Fifth and the Reeds, the Stopped Pipes, as well as syncopations and suspensions, in such manner that the Congregation can take the organ as the basis of good harmony and unison tone, and thus sing devoutly and give praise and thanks to the Most High.[47]

In a similar fashion, Christoph Graupner, in the preface to his Darmstadt *Choral-Buch* (1728), notes that chorale accompaniments are "best played simply and plainly, so that

46. BDOK V, 259 (no. 259); OBH, 5.

47. NBR, 67 (no. 48); BDOK II, 50–51 (no. 63): " . . . lieget ihm ob . . . 4.) Sich befleißigen, so wohl die ordentliche, als von denen HE. *Ministerialibus* vorgeschriebene *Choral*-Gesänge vor- und nach denen Sonn- und Fest-Tages Predigten, auch unter der *Communion, item* zur *Vesper* und *vigilien* Zeit, langsam ohne sonderbahres *coloriren* mit vier und fünff Stimmen und dem *Principal* andächtig einzuschlagen, und mit iedem *versicul* die andern Stimmen iedersmahl abzuwechseln, auch zur *quintaden* und Schnarr wercke, das Gedackte, wie auch die *syncopationes* und Bindungen dergestalt zu *adhibiren*, daß die eingepfarrete Gemeinde die Orgel zum *Fundamente* einer guten *Harmonie* und gleichstimmigen Thones sezen, darinn andächtig singen, und dem Allerhöchsten dancken und loben möge." In any event Bach never signed the document. However, the contract for the same position that W. F. Bach signed on April 16, 1746, included the same passage verbatim: see [Friedrich Chrysander], "Johann Sebastian Bach und Sein Sohn Friedemann Bach," *Jahrbücher für Musikalische Wissenschaft* 2 (1867): 243.

the congregation can hear the melody with excellent clarity."[48] Johann Daniel Müller reiterated this position in a new edition of the *Hessen-Hanauisches Choralbuch* in 1754. A noted string virtuoso, organist, and court musician in Darmstadt and Frankfurt—and later radical Pietist—who in 1735 spent some time with Bach in Leipzig,[49] Müller inveighs in this volume's preface "against the popular view that the art of the organist undermines rather than promotes [congregational] singing." Thus in his *Choralbuch*

> the [figured] basses have been set with all diligence so that they should not be overly chromatic, following the opinion of the highly-regarded Herr Capellmeister Graupner . . . because a chorale must be played completely naturally and tidily without exaggerated artistry, so that the congregation can hear the melody with excellent clarity."[50]

In 1787 a new edition of the *Hamburgisches Gesangbuch* was issued.[51] Later that year Diederich Christian Aumann, organist of the Heilige Dreyeinigkeitskirche in Hamburg, issued a *Choralbuch* containing 104 melodies with figured bass,[52] and Carl Philipp Emmanuel Bach issued, in the same format and from the same publisher, a small supplement of fourteen new melodies with figured bass that he had composed for the new *Gesangbuch*.[53] On the reverse of the title page appears this advice:

48. " . . . ist wohl das allerbeste, wenn der Choral ganz simpel und schlecht gespielt wird, daß die Gemeine die Melodie fein deutlich hören kann." Christoph Graupner, *Neu vermehrtes Darmstädtisches Choral-Buch: In welchen nicht alleine bishero gewöhnliche so wohl alt als neue Lieder enthalten, sondern auch noch beydentheils aus mehrern Gesang-Büchern ein Zusatz geschehen* ([Darmstadt]: [s.n.], 1728), [iv]. In this particular section of the preface, Graupner is speaking of chorale preludes, while Müller is addressing the issue of chorale accompaniment.

49. BDOK V, 208 (no. C 757a).

50. "Die Bässe hat man mit allem Fleiß nicht allzu *chromatisch* gesetzt, weilen man mit dem wohl belobten Herrn Cappell-Meister Graupner dafür hält, daß die übrige vermeynte Kunst der Organisten des Gesänge mehr verdirbt als befördet, und daß ein *Choral* gantz natürlich und ordentlich ohne übertriebene Künsteley müsse gespielet werden, damit die Gemeine die Melodie fein deutlich vernehmen könne." Johann Daniel Müller, *Vollständiges Hessen-Hanauisches Choralbuch, welches so wohl die Melodien der 150 Psalmen Davids, als anderer in beyden evangelischen Kirchen unsers Deutschlands bisher eingeführten alten und neuen Lieder in sich fasset: Zum allgemeinen Nutzen für Kirchen und Schulen, auch Privat-Andachten auf eine gantz neue Art eingerichtet und mit einem dazu nöthigen Vorbericht* (Frankfurt am Main: Stock, 1754), sig. ** verso. The last sentence is taken almost verbatim from Graupner's 1728 preface.

51. *Neues Hamburgisches Gesangbuch zum öffentlichen Gottesdienste und zur häuslichen Andacht ausgefertiget von dem Hamburgischen Ministerio* (Hamburg: Meyn, 1787). Preface dated January 26, 1787.

52. *Choral-Buch für das neue Hamburgische Gesangbuch: Herausgegeben von Diederich Christian Aumann, Organist Adjunctus der heiligen Dreyeinigkeits-Kirche in St. Georg* (Hamburg: Schniebes, 1787).

53. Carl Philipp Emanuel Bach, *Neue Melodien zu einigen Liedern des neuen hamburgischen Gesangbuchs: Nebst einigen Berichtigungen* ([Hamburg]: Herold and Schniebes, 1787).

> So that congregations can learn to sing together the new melodies freely and easily, the organists will do well, when, from the beginning, they support these melodies with moderate intervals, playing the prescribed and straightforward harmonies firmly and without affectation.[54]

Interestingly, this supplement of melodies with figured bass appeared in the same year as the final volume of Sebastian Bach's *Vierstimmige Choralgesänge* (Leipzig: Breitkopf, 1784–1787). The latter were called *Choralgesänge* rather than a collected *Choralbuch*, perhaps in order to emphasize the fact that these chorale settings were different from the keyboard versions necessary for accompanying congregational singing.[55] Indeed, printed and manuscript *Choralbücher* from this time witness consistently to a more restrained style of harmonization: simplified isometric melodies with sparsely figured basses are found in the *Choralbücher* published by Graupner, Telemann, Dretzel, and König.[56] The similarity between the settings in these published chorale anthologies and those in the Sibley *Choralbuch* raises the question whether the latter, too, might have been intended for publication.

In any case, the Sibley *Choralbuch* clearly fits within the tradition of simple organ accompaniments for congregational chorales in the eighteenth century. When Spitta posited an organ *Choralbuch* by Bach, he likely assumed that it would have been full of highly developed, harmonically rich settings of familiar melodies—that is, an anthology representing the finest settings that Bach was able to produce. The Sibley

54. "Anmerkung: Damit die Gemeinen die neuen Melodien leicht und bald mitsinging lernen, werden die Herrn Organisten wohl thun, wenn sie im Anfange diese aus leichten Intervallen gesetzte Melodien mit der vorgeschriebenen und untergelegten leichten Harmonien stark und ungekünstelt mitspielen." Bach, *Neue Melodien*, sig. A1v. Dated: "Hamburg, den 30sten Julius, 1787." Signed: "C. P. E. Bach."

55. The vocal style of the *Vierstimmige Choralgesänge* had commercial consequences: "The first editions of the chorales sold poorly and were controversial even among admirers, who questioned their style and utility while praising their creator's mastery of *Harmonie*." Matthew Dirst, *Engaging Bach: The Keyboard Legacy from Marpurg to Mendelssohn* (Cambridge: Cambridge University Press, 2012), 35.

56. Sparsely figured melodies can be found in Bach's Schemelli settings, such as BWV 471, or with no figures at all, as in BWV 451. There are many manuscript *Choralbücher* that have similar isometric melodies with meager figured basses. Not all are recorded, and significant examples keep coming to light. One notable recent discovery is the *Meiningisches Bachisches Choral-Buch*, dating from some time before 1750. Christine Blanken of the Bach Archiv, Leipzig, is preparing an article on the document, to be published in a forthcoming issue of the *Bach-Jahrbuch*; see *Johann Sebastian Bach: The Complete Organ Works*, I/1A: Pedagogical Works, edited by George B. Stauffer (Colfax: Leupold, 2012), xxxiii and xliv. On the Graupner volume, see n48 herewith; see also Georg Philipp Telemann, *Fast allgemeines Evangelisch-Musicalisch Lieder-Buch* (Hamburg: Stromer, 1730); Cornelius Heinrich Dretzel, *Des Evangelischen Musikalische Harmonie; oder, Evangelisches Choral-Buch* (Nuremburg: Endter, 1731); and Johann Balthasar König, *Harmonischer Lieder-Schatz; oder, Allgemeines Evangelisches Choral-Buch* (Frankfurt: [König], 1738).

Choralbuch is clearly not this, though some of its settings contain highly developed harmonic sequences, especially at final cadences, a feature that is not common in other contemporary *Choralbücher*, either printed or manuscript. Instead of being a collection of chorale settings "of rare originality and power" (to use Spitta's words), it is rather a more basic anthology of chorale harmonizations.

And that seems to have been exactly what Bach intended. In a letter to Forkel, dated January 13, 1775, Carl Philipp Emanuel wrote that his father's pupils

> had to begin their studies by learning pure four-part thorough bass. From this he went to chorales; first he added the basses to them himself, and they had to invent the alto and tenor. Then he taught them to devise the basses themselves.[57]

Does this mean that Bach wrote out melodies with figured basses independently for every organ pupil who came along? I think not. Given the constant stream of organists who came to study with him, and given his busy daily life, he would not have had time to parcel out individual figured bass chorales to each pupil. It seems much more likely that he prepared an anthology of figured bass chorales with basic harmonizations as the starting point—not the end point—of his pupils' studies. Thus at the beginning of their association with Bach, each pupil had either to copy out these basic chorales or to pay someone to make a copy (recall, for example, Johann Heinrich Gräbner's remark that his son's two years of study with Bach was at "no small cost" to himself).[58] When the pupil had such a manuscript in his possession, Bach could then assign various melodies, with his bass-lines and figures, in order for the pupil to create appropriate alto and tenor parts. Then, as pupils became proficient, they could create alternative bass-lines as well as inner parts for chorales.[59] One was expected to be able to harmonize a melody in multiple ways. Repeated use of the same melody in the Sibley *Choralbuch*, for example, typically occurs in a different key from the melody's previous iteration, with an alternative bass-line and different figures (see table 2). The Schemelli *Gesangbuch* follows the same principle: when no notation is provided, Bach uses a letter code to indicate the key in which a particular chorale melody should be played and sung; if

57. NBR, 399 (no. 395), BDOK III, 289 (no. 803): "Den Anfang musten seine Schüler mit der Erlernung des reinen 4stimmigen Generalbaßes machen. Hernach gieng er mit ihnen an die Choräle; setzte erstlich selbst den Baß dazu, u. den Alt u. den Tenor musten sie selbst erfinden. Alsdenn lehrte er sie selbst Bäße machen."

58. See note 26 herewith.

59. In a section on alternative basses in accompanying chorales, Adlung disparages the organist who uses only the same bass-line, as if one would wear only one coat throughout the year ("ein schlechter Spieler, der nur einen Baß wüste, wie Dir das ganze Jahr über nur einen Rock an sich trägt"). Adlung, *Anleitung*, 679 (§ 340).

the melody appears more than once, it is frequently assigned a different key.[60] At least two of Bach's pupils are known to have adopted a similar pedagogy of providing pupils with alternative basses and figures: Kittel and Kirnberger, both of whom declare that they were only passing on what they had learned from Bach.[61]

To summarize: the Sibley *Choralbuch* looks very much like an anthology either made by or for an organ pupil at the beginning of his studies with Bach, though it may not have come directly from Bach but rather indirectly via one of his pupils, and therefore could be a copy of a copy. This source served, in other words, as a workbook for learning how to create four-part settings. But it had a double usefulness: Bach could assign particular chorale melodies for the pupil to work on as test pieces, while the anthology could serve to accompany chorale singing at services. The aim was for the pupil to become more proficient, by composing alternative bass-lines with appropriate harmonies and ultimately by improvising such settings.

60. See Robin A. Leaver, "Letter Codes Relating to Pitch and Key for Chorale Melodies and Bach's Contributions to the Schemelli Gesangbuch," *Bach: The Journal of the Riemenschneider Bach Institute* 45, no. 1 (2014): 15–33.

61. Kittel's pedagogical manuscript is in the possession of Professor Yo Tomita: see Robin A. Leaver, "Suggestions for Future Research into Bach and the Chorale: Aspects of Repertoire, Pedagogy, Theory, and Practice," *Bach: The Journal of the Riemenschneider Bach Institute* 42, no. 2 (2011): 58–59. See also Johann Christian Kittel, *Der angehende praktische Organist* (Erfurt: Beyer and Maring, 1803–1808; reprint, Wiesbaden: Breitkopf and Härtel, 1986). Kirnberger's chorale pedagogy may be seen in Musikbibliothek der Stadt Leipzig. Ms. III/6/82a, 1 (see Leaver, "Suggestions for Future Research," 62). See also Johann Philipp Kirnberger, *Die Kunst des reinen Satzes in der Musik* (Berlin: Decker u. Hartung, 1776–1779; reprint, Hildesheim: Olms, 2010), 2:3–40.

Table 1. Contents of "Sebastian Bach's Choral-Buch"

Page	*Associated Text*	*Zahn*	*Alternatives*
1	Nun komm, der Heiden Heiland	1174	
2	Meine Seel erhebt den Herren	HDEKM I/1,499	
3	Gelobet sei der Herr, der Gott Israel	HDEKM I/1,488	
4	Von Adams her so lange Zeit	350	= Erhalt uns, Herr, bei deinem Wort
5	Menschenkind merk eben	3294	= Gott, durch deine Güte = Gottes Sohn ist kommen
6	Gottes Sohn ist kommen	3294	
7	Christum wir sollen loben schon	297	
8	Gelobet seist du, Jesu Christ	1947	
9	Vom Himmel hoch, da komm ich her	346	
10	Vom Himmel kam der Engel Schar	346	= Vom Himmel hoch da komm ich her
11	Puer natus in Bethlehem	192b	= Ein Kind geborn zu Bethlehem
12–13	Da Christus geboren war [Freuten]	4816	= Singen wir aus Herzensgrund
	Da Christus geboren war [sammelt]	4816	
14–15	Freuet euch, ihr Christen alle, freue sich	7880a	
16–17	Der Tag der ist so freudenreich	7870	
18–19	In dulci Jubilo	4897	
20	Gelobet seist du, Jesu Christ	1947	
21	Lobt Gott, ihr Christen all zugleich	198	= Kommt her, ihr lieben Schwesterlein
22	Wir Christenleut	2072	
23	Laßt uns alle fröhlich sein	1161	
24–25	Ermuntre dich, mein schwacher Geist	5741	= Du Lebensfürst, Herr Jesu Christ
26	Ein Kindelein so löbelich	7870	= Der Tag der ist so freudenreich
28	Freuet euch, ihr lieben Christen all	5375	
29	Kyrie, Gott Vater in Ewigkeit	8600	
30	Christe, aller Welt Trost	8600	
31	Kyrie, Gott Heiliger Geist	8600	
32	Allein Gott in der Höh sei Ehr	4457	
33	Helft mir Gottes Güte preisen	5267	
34–35	Jesu, nun sei gepreiset	8477a	
36	Was fürchtst du, Fiend Herodes, sehr	297	= Christum wir sollen loben schon
37	Mit Fried und Freud ich fahr dahin	3986	
38	O Lamm Gottes, unschuldig	4361a	
39	Christe du Lamm Gottes	58	
40–41	Christus, der uns selig macht	6283	
42–43	Christus, der uns selig macht	6283	
44	Christe, der du bist Tag und Licht	343	
45	Hilf, Gott, dass mir's gelinge	4329	
46	Da Jesus an dem Kreuze stund	1706	= In dich hab ich gehoffet, Herr

Page	*Associated Text*	*Zahn*	*Alternatives*
47	Jesu Leiden, Pein und Tod	6288b	= Jesu Kreuz, Leiden und Pein
48	Herzliebster Jesu	983	
49	O Haupt voll Blut und Wunden	5385a	= Herzlich tut mich verlangen
50	O Traurigkeit, o Herzeleid	1915	
51	O Welt, sieh hier dein Leben	2293b	= Nun ruhen aller Wälder = O Welt, ich muß dich lassen
52–53	Ach [O] wir armen Sünder	8187h	
54–55	O Mensch, bewein dein sünde groß	8303	= Es sind doch selig alle
56	Ach stirbt denn so mein allerliebstes Leben	1831a	= Ach Gott, erhör mein Seufzen
57	Jesu, meines Lebens Leben	6804	= Wachet doch, erwacht, ihr Schläfer = Jesu, der du meiner Seele
58	Der am Kreuz ist meine Liebe	6551a	= Werde munter, mein Gemüte
59	Christ lag in Todesbanden	7012a	
60	Jesus Christus, unser Heiland, d.d.T	1978	
61	Erschienen ist der herrliche Tag	1743	
62	Erstanden ist der herrlich Christ	288	= Surrexit Christus hodie
63	Surrexit Christus hodie	291	
64–65	Christ ist erstanden	8584	
66–67	Heut triumphiret Gottes Sohn	2585	
68	Erschienen ist der heilige Christ	1743	= Erschienen ist der herrlich Tag
69	Nun freuet euch, Gottes Kinder all	364	= Ihr lieben Christen, freut euch nun
70–71	Christ fuhr gen Himmel	8586	
72	Gen Himmel aufgefahren ist	188a	= Coelos ascendit hodie
73	Komm, Gott Schöpfer, heiliger Geist	295	
74–75	Komm, Heiliger Geist, Herre Gott	7445a	
76	Nun bitten wir den Heiligen Geist	2029	
77	Spiritus sancti gratia [... simil omnia]	370b/c	= Wir danken dir, Herr Jesu Christ
78	Kyrie, Gott Vater in Ewigkeit	8600	
79	Christe, aller Welt Trost	8600	
80	Kyrie, Gott Heiliger Geist	8600	
[NB pp. 81-84 repeat pp. 77–80]			
81	Spiritus sancti gratia [... simil omnia]	370b/c	= Wir danken dir, Herr Jesu Christ
82	Kyrie, Gott Vater in Ewigkeit	8600	
83	Christe, aller Welt Trost	8600	
84	Kyrie, Gott Heiliger Geist	8600	
85	Allein Gott in der Hoh sei Ehr	4457	
86–87	Gott, der Vater, wohn uns bei	8507	
88	Herr Gott, dich loben aller wir	368	= Ihr Knecht des Herren allzugleich
89	Herr Gott, erhalt uns für und für	439	= Ach bleib bei uns, Herr Jesu Christ
90	Dies sind die heilgen zehn Gebot	1951	
91	Vater unser im Himmelreich	2561	
92–93	Vater unser im Himmelreich	2561	
94–95	Christ unser Herr zum Jordan kam	7246	= Es wolle uns Gott gnädig sein

Page	Associated Text	Zahn	Alternatives
96–97	Wir glauben all an einen Gott	7971	
98–99	Wir glauben all an einen Gott	7971	
100–1	Wir glauben all an einen Gott	7971	
102–3	Wir glauben all an einen Gott	7971	
104	Ach Herr mich armen Sünder	5385a	= Herzlich tut mich verlangen = O Haupt voll Blut und Wunden
105	Befiehl du deine Wege	5385a	= Herzlich tut mich verlangen = O Haupt voll Blut und Wunden
106	Straf mich nicht in deinem Zorn	6274a	
107	Herr ich habe misgehandelt	3695	
108	Erbarm dich mein o Herre Gott	5851	
109	Aus tiefer Noth schrei ich zu dir	4437	
110	Aus der Tieffe rufe ich	1218	
111	Ach Gott und Herr	2051	
112	Wo soll ich fliehen hin	2164	= Auf meinen lieben Gott
113	Ach, was soll ich Sünder machen?	3573b	
114–15	Allein zu dir, Herr Jesu Christ	7292b	
116	Herr Jesu Christ, du höchstes Gut	4486	= Wenn mein Stündlein vorhanden ist
117	Durch Adams Fall ist gantz verderbt	7549	
118	Es ist das Heil uns kommen her	4430	
119	Nun freut euch, lieben Christen gmein	4427	
120	Jesus Christus, unser Heiland, der von uns	1576	
121	Schmücke dich, o liebe Seele	6923	
122–23	Gott sei gelobet und gebenedeiet	8078	
124–25	Gott sei gelobet und gebenedeiet	8078	
126–27	Gott sei gelobet und gebenedeiet	8078	
128	O Jesu, du mein Bräutigam	423	= Herr Jesu Christ, wahr Mensch und Gott
129	Schatz über aller Schätze	5404a	= Valet will ich dir geben
130–38	Herr Gott, dich loben wir	8652	
139–47	Herr Gott, dich loben wir	8652	
148–49	Nun lob, mein Seel, den Herren	8244	
150	Nun laßt uns Gott dem Herren	159	
151	Wie schön leuchtet der Morgenstern	8359	
152	Nun danket alle Gott	5142	
153	Ich dank dir, lieber Herre	5354	
154	Aus meines Herzens Grunde	5269	
155	Wach auf, mein Herz, und singe	159	= Nun laßt uns Gott dem Herren
156	Ich dank dir schon durch deinen Sohn	247	
157	Das walt mein Gott	4217	
158	Gott des Himmels und der Erden	3614	
159	Der Tag vertreibt die finstre Nacht	51	
160	O Christe, Morgensterne	1661b	

Page	*Associated Text*	*Zahn*	*Alternatives*
161	Christe, der du bist Tag un Licht	343	= Christe qui lux es et dies
162	Christ, du bist der helle Tag	384	
163	Nun sich der Tag geendet hat	212	
164	Nun ruhen aller Wälder	2293	= O Welt, ich muß dich lassen
165	Werde munter, mein Gemüte	6551a	
166	Hinunter ist der Sonnen Schein	305	= Wo Gott zum Haus nicht gibt sein Gunst
167	In dieser Abend Stunde	1661b	= O Christe Morgenstern
168	Mein Augen schließ ich jetzt	1067	
169	Der lieben Sonne Licht und Pracht		
170	Danket dem Herren denn er ist sehr ...	12	= Vitiam quae faciunt
171	Lobet den Herren denn er ist sehr freundlich	975	
172–73	Singen wir aus Herzensgrund	4816d	
174	Herr Gott nun sei gepreiset	4297a	= Herr Christ, der einig Gotts Sohn
175	Ach Gott vom Himmel sieh darein	4431	
176	Es spricht der Unweisen Mund wohl	4436	
177	Ein feste burg ist unser Gott	7377	
178–79	Es wolle Gott uns gnädig sein	7247	
180	Wär Gott nicht uns dieser Zeit	4434	
181	Wo Gott der Herr nicht bei uns hält	4441	
182–83	Treuer Wächter Israel	4816d	= Singen wir aus Herzenzsgrund
184	Erhalt uns, Herr, bei deinem Wort	350	
185	Verleih uns Frieden gnädiglich	1945a	
186	Gib unserm Fürsten	1945b	
187	Ach bleib bei uns, Herr Jesu Christ	439	= Herr Gott, erhalt uns für und für
188	O Herre Gott, dein göttlich Wort	5690	
189	Ach bleib mit deiner Gnade	134	= Christus der ist mein Leben
190	Herr Jesu Christ, dich zu uns wend	624	
191	Herr Jesu Christ, dich zu uns wend	624	
192	Liebster Jesu, wir sind hier	3498b	
193	Kommt her zu mir, spricht Gottes Sohn	2496c	
194	O Gott, du frommer Gott	5144	
195	Ich ruf zu dir, Herr Jesu Christ	7400	
196	Warum solt ich mich denn grämen	6468	
197	Du o schönes Weltgebäude	6773	= Du geballtes Weltgebäude
198	Was mein Gott will, daß gescheh allzeit	7568	
199	Wer nur den lieben Gott läßt walten	2778	
200	Herr, wie du wilt, so schicks mit mir	4438	= Aus tiefer Not schrei ich zu dir
201	Wo Gott zum Haus nicht giebt sein Gunst	305	
202	Wohl dem der in Gottesfurcht steht	298	
203	In allen meinen Taten	2282	
204	Mein Jesu dem die Seraphinen	5991	
205	Gott Vater der du deine Sonn	380	

Page	*Associated Text*	*Zahn*	*Alternatives*
206–7	Herr Gott Vater, Schöpfer aller dinge	8643	
208	Wenn wir in höchsten Nöthen sein	394	
209	O großer Gott von Macht	5105a	
210–11	An Wasserflüssen Babylon	7663	
212	Du Friedefürst, Herr Jesu Christ	4373	
213	Ach lieben Christen seid getrost	4441a	= Wo Gott der Herr nicht bei uns hält
214	Warum betrübst du dich mein Herz	1689	
215	Verzage nicht, o frömmer Christ	1712	
216	In dich hab ich gehoffet, Herr	2461	
217	Ich heb mein Augen sehnlich auf	542	
218	Zion klagt mit Angst und Schmertzen	6543	= Wie nach einer Wasserquelle
219	Ach Gott erhör mein Seufzen	1831a	
220	Was Gott tut, das ist wohlgetan	5629	
221	Sollt es gleich bisweilen scheinen	1347	= Singet nun mit großem Schalle
222	Von Gott will ich nicht lassen	5264b	
223	Auf meinen lieben Gott	2164	
224–25	Wer Gott vertraut, hat wohl gebaut	8207	
226–27	Ach Gott wird denn mein Leid	5206b	
228–29	Ich laß dich nicht	7455	
230	Jesu der du meine Seele	6804	= Wachet doch, erwacht, ihr Schläfer
231	Jesu, meine Freude	8032	
232	Nicht so traurig nicht so sehr	3336	
233	Sollt ich meinem Gott nicht singen	7891	= Jesu, du mein liebstes Leben
234–35	Welt ade ich bin dein müde	6531	
236–37	Mitten wir im Leben sind	8502	
238	Ach wie flüchtig, ach wie nichtig	1887b	
239	Alle Menschen müssen sterben		
240	Ich hab mein Sach Gott heimgestellt	1679	
241	Ich weiß ein Blümlein hübsch und fein	1679	= Ich hab mein Sach Gott heimgestellt
242	Meinen Jesum laß ich nicht	3458	
243	Herr [O] Jesu Christ, meins Lebens Licht	533a	
244	Herr Jesu Christ, wahr Mensch und Gott	533b	
245	Nun laßt uns den Leib begraben	352	
246–47	Herzlich lieb hab ich dich, o Herr	8326	
248	Machs mit mir, Gott, nach deiner Güt	2383	
249	Freu dich sehr, o meiner Seele	6543	
250	Es ist nun aus mit meinem Leben	6125	
251	So wünsch ich nun ein gute Nacht	4410	
252	O wie selig seid ihr doch, ihr Frommen	1583	
253	Gott hat das Evangelium	1788	
254–55	Ach Gott thu dich erbarmen	7228	
256–57	Wachet auf, rufft uns die Stimmen	8405	

Page	Associated Text	Zahn	Alternatives
258	Es ist gewißlich an der Zeit	4429	= Nun freut euch, lieben Christen gmein
259	Es wird schier der letzte Tag herkommen	1423	
260	O Ewigkeit, du Donnerwort	5820	
261	Jesu meines Herzens Freude	4798c	
262	Meinen Jesum laß ich nicht	3458	
263	Herr, der du vormahls hast dein Land	4434	= Wär Gott nicht mit uns dieser Zeit
264	Ich erhebe Herr zu dir	3336	= Nicht so traurig, nicht so sehr
265	Du sagst ich bin ein Christ	5145	= O Gott, du großer Gott
266–67	Lasset uns den Herren preisen	7901	= Sollt ich meinem Gott nicht singen
268	Du Lebensbrodt, Herr Jesu Christ	4429	= Nun freut euch, lieben Christen gmein
269	Kommt her ihr Menschenkinder	2293	= Nun ruhen aller Wälder
270	Herr Gott du kennest meine Tage	2778	= Wer nur den lieben Gott läßt walten
271	Ei sage meine Seele	4297a	= Herr Christ, der einig Gotts Sohn
272–73	Du Lebensfürst Herr Jesu Christ	5741	= Ermuntre dich, mein schwacher Geist
274	Schaffs mit mir Gott nach deinem Willen	2778	= Wer nur den lieben Gott läßt walten
275	Wer sich auf seine Schwachheit steurt	7549	= Durch Adams Fall ist ganz verderbt
276–77	Eins ist not! Ach Herr, dies Eine	7127	
278	Mein Gott dein heilig Bibelbuch	2383	
279	Gott du hast es so beschlossen	Not in Zahn	
280	Jesu Jesu laß dein Leiden	Not in Zahn	
281	Gott sei uns gnädig und barmherzig	HDEKM I/1,499	= Meine Seel erhebt den Herren
282–83	Gott sei uns gnädig und barmherzig	HDEKM I/1,499	= Meine Seel erhebt den Herren
284	Brich entzwei mein armes Herze	7108	
285	Herr Christ, der einig Gotts Sohn	4297a	

Table 2. Alternative Settings in the Sibley *Choralbuch*

Zahn Nos.		*Page Nos.*
159	Nun laßt uns Gott dem Herren	150, 155
297	Christum wir sollen loben schon	7, 36
305	Hinunter ist der Sonnenschein	166, 201
343	Christe, der du bist Tag und Licht	44, 161
346	Vom Himmel hoch da komm ich her	9, 10
350	Erhalt uns Herr bey deinem wort	4, 184
533	Herr [O] Jesu Christ meins lebens licht	243, 244
624	Herr Jesu Christ dich zu uns wend	190, 191
1661b	O Christe Morgenstern	160, 167
1679	Ich hab mein sach Gott heimgestellet	240, 241
1743	Erschienen ist der herrlich tag	61, 68
1831a	Ach stirbt denn so mein allerliebstes leben	56, 219
1947	Gelobet seist du, Jesu Christ	8, 20
2164	Wo soll ich fliehen hin	112, 223
2282	In allen meinen Thaten	51, 164, 203, 269
2383	Machs mit mir Gott nach deiner Gut	248, 278
2561	Vater unser im Himmelreich	91, 92-93
2778	Wer nur den lieben Gott laßt walten	199, 270
3294	Menschen Kind merk eben	5, 6
3336	Nicht so traurig nicht so sehr	232, 264
3458	Meinen Jesum laß ich nicht	242, 262
4297a	Herr Gott nun sey gepreiset	174, 271, 285
4429	Es ist gewißlich an der Zeit	258, 268
4441a	Wo Gott der Herr nicht bey uns halt	181, 213
4457	Allein Gott in der Höh sey Ehr	32, 85
4816	Da Christus gebohren war freuten	12-13, 172-73, 182-83
5385a	O Haupt voll Blut und Wunden	49, 104, 105
5741	Ermuntre dich, mein schwacher Geist	24-25, 272-73
6543	Zion klagt mit Angst und schmertzen	218, 249
6551	Der am Kreuz ist meine liebe	58, 165
6804	Jesu der du meine Seele	57, 230
7445	Komm, Heiliger Geist, Herre Gott	74-75, 228-29
7549	Durch Adams fall ist gantz verderbt	117, 275
7870	Der Tag der ist so freudenreich	16-17, 26
7971	Wir glauben all an einen Gott	96-97, 98-99, 100-101, 102-3
8078	Gott sei gelobet und gebenedeiet	122-23, 124-25, 126-27
8600	Kyrie, Gott Vater in Ewigkeit	29-31, 78-80, [82-84]
8652	Herr Gott dich loben wir	130-38, 139-47

Miscellaneous Organ Trios from Bach's Leipzig Workshop

George B. Stauffer

One of the great mysteries about the working methods of Johann Sebastian Bach is how the composer created his encyclopedic collections. In some cases we can observe a long period of preparation, when Bach took up a new genre, explored its potential in various works, and then put together a unique, definitive compendium that summarizes its possibilities. Take the *Well-Tempered Clavier*, for instance. We can trace Bach's codification of the prelude-fugue pair in organ works from the Arnstadt, Mühlhausen, and Weimar years; his assembling of twenty-four preludes and fughettas around 1720; his use of the first twelve preludes in the *Clavierbüchlein für Wilhelm Friedemann Bach* about a year later; and finally his expansion and revision of the earlier texts to create, around 1722 or 1723, a beautiful fair-copy album, titled "Das wohltemperirte Clavier," with twenty-four prelude-fugue pairs in a rising chromatic, major-minor sequence.[1]

In other instances, however, encompassing collections seem to have appeared out of the blue, without any of the expected gestatory steps. We can observe this phenomenon in the Six Sonatas and Partitas for Unaccompanied Violin, BWV 1001–1006; their companion work, the Six Suites for Unaccompanied Cello, BWV 1007–1012; and the "Goldberg" Variations, BWV 988. In each case, Bach produced, in a relatively short span of time, an encyclopedic compendium that is a fully formed masterpiece—a work quite unlike anything before or after—and most remarkably, seemingly without preparatory studies.[2] This makes the creation of an encyclopedic compendium all the more remarkable.

1. NBA V/6.1, KB (edited by Alfred Dürr; 1989), 132–96.

2. NBA VI/1, KB (edited by Günter Hausswald and Rudolf Gerber, 1958), 62–64; NBA VI/2, KB (edited by Hans Eppstein, 1990), 31–32; and NBA V/2, KB (edited by Christoph Wolff and Walter Emery, 1981), 109–13.

The Six Trio Sonatas

Remarkable, indeed, are the Six Trio Sonatas for Organ, BWV 525–530, which appear to fit into the second creative pattern, since they were not preceded by similar three-movement free organ trios. We know at least a few details about the collection's origin. Forkel tells us that the Six Sonatas were assembled for the use of Bach's oldest son, Wilhelm Friedemann, to give final polish to his organ technique:

> Six Sonatas, or Trios, for two claviers and obbligato pedal. Bach composed them for his eldest son, Wilhelm Friedemann, who by practicing them prepared himself for becoming the great performer on the organ that he afterward was. It is impossible to say enough of their beauty. They were composed when the author was in his most mature age and may be considered as his chief work of this description.[3]

The watermark and handwriting of the autograph manuscript of the Six Sonatas, SBB-PK *Mus.ms. Bach P 271*, suggest that the collection was put together around 1730,[4] when Bach was "in his most mature age" and Friedemann was twenty years old and well on his way to becoming a virtuoso organist. Within three years Friedemann was named organist of St. Sophia's Church in Dresden, and it is likely that he carried a copy of the Six Sonatas with him as he took up his new post.[5]

In addition, we can observe traces of the Six Sonata's "prehistory." Early versions survive for four movements, and we can detect instrumental models for two others:[6]

Trio in E♭ Major, BWV 525/1a	→	Sonata 1 in E♭ Major, movement 1
Trio in D Minor, BWV 527/1a	→	Sonata 3 in D Minor, movement 1
Trio in D Minor, BWV 528/2a	→	Sonata 4 in E Minor, movement 2
Trio in A Minor, BWV 529/2a	→	Sonata 5 in C Major, movement 2

3. Johann Nicolaus Forkel, *Über Johann Sebastian Bachs Leben, Kunst und Kunstwerke* (Leipzig: Hoffmeister and Kühnel, 1802; reprint Kassel: Bärenreiter, 1999), 60; English translation from NBR, 471–72.

4. The watermark, No. 122 in NBA IX/1, appears in Bach's works from 1727 to 1731; Georg von Dadelsen, in *Beiträge zur Chronologie der Werke Johann Sebastian Bachs* (Trossingen: Hohner, 1958), 104, dates Bach's handwriting in *P 271* as ca.1730.

5. The second house copy of the Six Sonatas, *Mus. ms. Bach P 272* in the Berlin State Library, jointly written by Wilhelm Friedemann and Anna Magdalena Bach, displays a watermark, No. 121 in NBA IX/1, that appears in Bach's works from 1732 to 1735.

6. This list is limited to the variants that can be confirmed. It does not include the hypothetical variants proposed by Hans Klotz, in "Bachs Orgeln und seine Orgelmusik," *Die Musikforschung* 3 (1950), 196, and Dietrich Kilian, in NBA IV/7, KB (1988), 66–88. Kilian viewed the Trio in E-flat Major, BWV 525/1a, as an arrangement made after the completion of BWV 525/1 to accommodate an organ with a pedal compass of C-c′ (NBA IV/7, KB, 68–70). But aside from the pedal adjustments, the varied readings reflect early, less refined compositional decisions and suggest that BWV 525/1a is an early version of the movement.

Lost instrumental trio[7]	→	Sonata 3 in D Minor, movement 2
Sinfonia from Cantata 76, Part II	→	Sonata 4 in E Minor, movement 1

The roots of Bach's interest in the free organ trio and his broader compositional preparations for the Six Sonatas project are much less clear, however. The traditional view holds that Bach began composing free organ trios—that is, trios not based on a chorale melody—in Weimar, in conjunction with his first chorale trios. It was in Weimar that he wrote "most of his organ works," the obituary of 1754 tells us,[8] and it would not be illogical to assume that the roots of the Six Sonatas extend back to that period. There is no question that Bach composed a number of impressive chorale trios in Weimar, including three large pieces that ended up in the "Great Eighteen" Collection: "Trio super Herr Jesu Christ, dich zu uns wend," BWV 655a; "Nun komm, der Heiden Heiland," BWV 660a; and "Trio super Allein Gott in der Höh sei Ehr," BWV 664a. The free trios assigned to Weimar by one scholar or another include two of the Six Sonata variants—the Trio in D minor, BWV 528/2a and Trio in A Minor, BWV 529/2a—and the Trio in F Major ("Aria"), BWV 587.[9]

Recent source studies have brought the Weimar origins of the free trios into question,[10] however, and the notation and style of the pieces suggest a later line of development, as we shall see. The chorale trios sprang from hymn tunes: their thematic

7. A piece no longer extant but also used as the model for the middle movement of the Concerto in A Minor for Flute, Violin, Harpsichord, and Strings, BWV 1044. See Hans Epstein, "Grundzüge in J. S. Bachs Sonatenschaffen," *Bach-Jahrbuch* 55 (1969), 23.

8. BDOK III, no. 666; NBR, 300.

9. Walter Emery, *Notes on Bach's Organ Works* (London: Novello, 1957), book IV, 102 (BWV 528/2a); Dietrich Kilian in NBA IV/7, KB, 86 (BWV 529/2a); Peter Williams, *The Organ Music of J. S. Bach*, 2nd ed. (Cambridge: Cambridge University Press, 1983), 24 (BWV 528/2a); or Kerstin Delang, "Couperin—Pisendel—Bach: Überlegungen zur Echtheit und Datierung des Trios BWV 587 anhand eines Quellenfundes in der Sächsischen Landesbibliothek—Staats- und Universitätsbibliothek Dresden," *Bach-Jahrbuch* 93 (2007), 199 (BWV 587), for instance.

10. Hans-Joachim Schulze, in "'Das Stück in Goldpapier'—Ermittlungen zu einigen Bach-Abschriften des frühen 18. Jahrhunderts," *Bach-Jahrbuch* 64 (1978), 32, demonstrated that Johann Caspar Vogler's copies of the Trio in D Minor, BWV 527/1a, and Trio in A Minor, BWV 529/2a, date from Leipzig, ca. 1729, rather than Weimar; and Kirsten Beißwenger, in "Zur Chronologie der Notenhandschriften Johann Gottfried Walthers," in *Acht kleine Präludien und Studien über BACH—Festschrift für Georg von Dadelsen* (Wiesbaden: Breitkopf and Härtel, 1992), 29 and 38n47, showed that Johann Gottfried Walther's copy of the Trio in A Minor is derived from Vogler's and dates from Leipzig, after 1729, rather than Weimar. Both Dietrich Kilian and the present writer proposed that the pairing of the Trio in A Minor with the Prelude and Fugue in C Major, BWV 545, and the *Un poc' allegro* from Sonata 4 in E Minor, BWV 528/3, with the Prelude and Fugue in G Major, BWV 541, was a sign of Bach's interest in creating three-movement concerto forms in Weimar (see Dietrich Kilian, "Dreisätzige Fassungen

material, imitative treatment, and formal structure were determined by phrases of a chorale. The free trios, by contrast, had instrumental models: their thematic material, imitative treatment, and formal structure were derived from Italian trio writing. The fact that Bach does not seem to have taken up the instrumental trio until his Cöthen years, when he was required to produce chamber music for the court of Prince Leopold, hints at a post-Weimar origin for the free organ trios. A close review of the source materials and Bach's evolving compositional interests raises the possibility that he did not became interested in the free organ trio until Leipzig, and then chiefly during the five-year period leading up to the composition of the Six Sonatas—that is, between 1725 and 1730.

The Miscellaneous Free Trios

That Bach wrote other free organ trios is clear from Forkel's characterization of the Six Trio Sonatas as the composer's "*chief* work of this description" and his additional remark that "several individual pieces, which are still available here and there, may also be reckoned fine, though they do not equal the first mentioned."[11] Aside from the four Sonata variants, which are handed down as independent pieces,[12] there are six extant free organ trios attributed to Bach that may represent at least in part the "several others" to which Forkel refers:

Trio in C Minor, BWV 21/1a (after the Sinfonia from Cantata 21)
Trio in D Minor, BWV 583
Trio in G Minor, BWV 584 (after the aria "Ich will an den Himmel denken" from Cantata 166)
Trio in C Minor, BWV 585 (after Fasch, Trio Sonata in C Minor for Two Violins and Continuo)
Trio in G Major, BWV 586 (after Telemann, lost trio sonata?)
Trio in F Major ("Aria"), BWV 587 (after Couperin, Trio Sonata "La Convalescente")

Moreover, there are four additional free trios that are credited to Bach in the early sources but most likely stem from colleagues or students in his circle:

Bachscher Orgelwerke," in *Bach-Interpretationen*, edited by Martin Geck [Göttingen: Vandenhoeck and Ruprecht, 1969], 12–21, and George B. Stauffer, *The Organ Preludes of Johann Sebastian Bach* [Ann Arbor: UMI Research, 1980], 134). Beißwenger's findings, in particular, demonstrate that the pairings took place instead in Bach's circle in Leipzig around 1729.

11. Forkel, *Über Johann Sebastian Bachs Leben*, 60. "Chief" italicized for emphasis.

12. And in other combinations as well, in a complicated array. See NBA IV/7, KB, 66–88.

Concerto in E♭ Major, BWV 597
Trio in B Minor, BWV 790a (after Sinfonia 3 in D Minor, BWV 790)
Trio in C Major, BWV 1014/3a (after movement 3 of Sonata 1 in B Minor for Violin and Cembalo, BWV 1014)
Sonata in G Major, BWV 1039/1a, 2a, and 4a (after movements 1, 2, and 4 of the Sonata in G Major for Two Flutes and Continuo, BWV 1039, or its model)[13]

These ten miscellaneous free trios, which include transcriptions and original pieces, and the four variants from the Six Sonatas share common ties in the early sources—a striking fact unexplored in the literature.[14] The ties suggest that the trios may have formed a distinct repertory at one time, a repertory stemming from Bach's Leipzig workshop.

Before looking at the pieces themselves, we need to consider their interrelationships within the sources. Dietrich Kilian was the first to discern the one-time existence of a manuscript collection entitled "35 Orgeltrio's von Sebastian Bach," which seems to have been assembled in Leipzig at the time of Bach's death or shortly thereafter and sold in various forms by the Breitkopf publishing firm in the 1760s.[15] Breitkopf house copies were normally manuscripts and remained so, since they were used for copying purposes only. Two fragments of the Breitkopf collection survive today: the Grønland manuscript of 1795, containing seven pieces, and the Kühnel manuscript of ca. 1810, containing seventeen.[16] From these extracts we can conclude that "35 Orgeltrios" was a miscellany, containing both free and chorale trios.[17] As was com-

13. Only the arrangement of the fourth movement is cited in the Schmieder catalog, where it is listed as BWV 1027a, a variant of the Sonata in G Major for viola da gamba and harpsichord. All three organ transcriptions probably stem from a lost trio sonata that served as the model for both the gamba sonata and the Sonata in G Major for two flutes and continuo, BWV 1039. The text of the organ arrangements is much closer to that of the two-flute sonata than that of the gamba sonata, and as a consequence the movements are given the Schmieder number BWV 1039/1a, 2a, and 4a here.

14. The ties were not noted in the *Neue Bach-Ausgabe* because the pieces were addressed intermittently over a twenty-four-year period in three separate volumes by four different editors: NBA IV/7 (edited by Dietrich Kilian, 1984–1988), IV/8 (edited by Karl Heller, 1979–1980), and IV/11 (edited by Ulrich Bartels and Peter Wollny, 2003–2004). The miscellaneous free trios were never considered as a group.

15. NBA IV/7, KB, 58.

16. Copenhagen, Det Kongelige Bibliotek, Wayse Samling, *MU 9210.2685*, copied by the Copenhagen Justice Councillor Peter Grønland (1761–1825), and SBB-PK *Mus. ms. Bach P 1115*, copied by Ambrosius Kühnel (1770–1813), co-owner of Hoffmeister & Kühnel (the predecessor of C. F. Peters publishing firm in Leipzig). See NBA IV/KB, 53–54, and I/20, KB, 13 (on Peter Grønland).

17. Among others, the Schübler Chorales (in the order 1, 4, 2, 3, 5, 6), Canonic Variations on "Vom Himmel hoch" (in the order 1, 2, 5, 3, 4), and trios from the "Great Eighteen" Collection (*An*

mon at the time, the collection was probably assembled with an eye to the growing market for pedagogical materials: collections of organ trios became increasingly popular during the second half of the eighteenth century, as organized organ instruction became routine. The free trios that appear in both the Grønland and Kühnel manuscripts consist of three variants from the Six Sonatas—Trio in E♭ Major, BWV 525/1a; Trio in D Minor, BWV528/2a; and Trio in A Minor, BWV 529/2a—and the independent Trio in D Minor, BWV 583. This constellation raises the possibility that the early Sonata variants may have been grouped together at one time—perhaps in a composition workbook like those for the Art of Fugue[18] or the "Great Eighteen" Chorales[19]—and that the Trio in D Minor, BWV 583, may have been included with them (a point to which we shall return).

A second important source of the miscellaneous free trios, also not fully understood, is the series of mid-nineteenth-century editions issued by Gotthilf Wilhelm Körner (1809–1865): *Der Orgelfreund* (1842), *Sämmtliche Orgel-Compositionen von Joh. Sebast. Bach* (1848–1852), and *Höheres Orgel-Spiel* (c. 1850), among others. The *Sämmtliche Orgel-Compositionen* included two volumes of "Orgel-Trios von J. S. Bach" that contain the Trio in C Minor, BWV 21/1a; Trio in D Minor, BWV 528/2a; Trio in D Minor, BWV 583; Trio in G Minor, BWV 584; Trio in G Major, BWV 586; Trio in B Minor, BWV 790a; and Trio in C Major, BWV 1014/3a.[20] Both Alfred Dürr and Paul Brainard drew attention to the Körner editions when editing Cantatas 166 and 21 (*Wo gehest du hin?* and *Ich hatte viel Bekümmernis*, respectively) for the *Neue Bach Ausgabe*.[21] In each case

Wasserflüssen Babylon, BWV 653; *Nun komm, der Heiden Heiland*, BWV 661; and *Allein Gott in der Höh sei Ehr*, BWV 664b).

18. SBB-PK *Mus. ms. Bach P 200*, which Bach appears to have initiated around 1740, ten years before he brought the work to print.

19. SBB-PK *Mus. ms. Bach P 271*, which Bach appears to have initiated around 1739 to serve as a repository for revised versions of large Weimar chorale prelude settings, most probably with the intention of future publication.

20. In Heft 51 (BWV 1014/3a, 586, 583, and 790a) and Heft 52 (BWV 584, 528/2a, Kellner's Trio in D Major, and BWV 21/1a). See NBA IV/11, KB, 116 and 160. Körner sometimes printed pieces in more than one series, with the result that some trios appeared several times. The Trio in C Minor, BWV 21/1a, for instance, initially appeared in *Der Orgel-Freund* before being reprinted in the *Sämmtliche Orgel-Compositionen* series.

21. Alfred Dürr, "Verstummelt überlieferte Arien aus Kantaten J. S. Bachs," *Bach-Jahrbuch* 46 (1960), 40–42, and NBA I/12, KB (1960), 13 and 18–25; Paul Brainard, NBA I/16, KB (1984), 140–44. The ties between the Trio in G Minor, BWV 584, and Cantata 166 were first noticed (though incorrectly interpreted) by Reinhard Oppel in "Zur Tenorarie der 166. Kantate," *Bach-Jahrbuch* 6 (1909), 27–40.

the Körner publication gives a unique organ-trio arrangement that reflects lost source materials for the cantatas: the Trio in G Minor, BWV 584, based on the tenor aria "Ich will an den Himmel denken" from Cantata 166, displays an otherwise lost obbligato line from which Dürr was able to reconstruct the aria in its original form, with a violin obbligato; and the Trio in C Minor, BWV 21/1a, based on the Sinfonia from Cantata 21, reflects a lost D-minor version of the work that Bach appears to have performed in Hamburg in 1720.[22]

Despite the late date of his editions, Körner seems to have drawn on primary sources, long since disappeared, possibly from the hands of Bach's student Johann Christian Kittel through Kittel's own students Johann Immanuel Müller and Ludwig Ernst Gebhardi, with whom Körner studied in Erfurt.[23] Körner may also have been familiar with the "35 Orgeltrios" collection, given the fact that the Trio in D Minor, BWV 528/2a, and Trio in D Minor, BWV 583, appear in both the "35 Orgeltrios" and Körner's editions. The recent discovery of a copy of the Trio in C Minor, BWV 21/1a (plate 1), appended to a manuscript copy of the Six Sonatas written during Bach's lifetime,[24] greatly strengthens the case for this arrangement's authenticity and its close ties with the Six Sonatas. It also underscores anew the importance of the Körner editions.

The Trio in D Minor, BWV 527/1a; Trio in C Minor, BWV 585; Trio in G Major, BWV 586; Concerto in E♭ Major, BWV 597; and Sonata in G Major, BWV 1039/4a, are transmitted in the Mempell-Preller Collection, assembled by Johann Gottlieb Preller (1727–1786) between 1743 and 1749 by adding his copies to those made in the 1730s by Bach enthusiast Johann Nicholas Mempell (1713–1747).[25] Mempell may have studied with Johann Peter Kellner (1705–1772), who had direct contact with Bach. Reported only in 1904,[26] the Mempell-Preller Collection is one of the most important

22. BC, Version A99b. See also Christoph Wolff, *Johann Sebastian Bach: The Learned Musician*, rev. ed. (New York: Norton, 2013), 213–14.

23. NBA IV/5–6, KB (edited by Dietrich Kilian, 1978), 257–58.

24. The anonymous manuscript, Schwerin, Landesbibliothek Mecklenburg-Vorpommern, *Mus. 888a*, surfaced only in 2003. It contains a complete copy of the Six Sonatas, derived from the text of the collection during Bach's lifetime (including some, but not all, of the additions made to *P 271* by the composer before 1750), as well as the Trio in C Minor, written by the same scribe. See NBA IV/11, 222 (Nachtrag), and the discussion in *Johann Sebastian Bach: The Complete Organ Works*, edited by George B. Stauffer (Colfax, N.C.: Wayne Leupold, 2010–present), vol. 7 (Six Trio Sonatas and Miscellaneous Trios), 150–51.

25. Hans-Joachim Schulze, "Wie entstand die Bach-Sammlung Mempell-Preller?" *Bach-Jahrbuch* 60 (1974), 104–22, and *Studien zur Bach-Überlieferung im 18. Jahrhundert* (Leipzig: Peters, 1984), 69–88.

26. Max Seiffert, "Neue Bach-Funde," *Jahrbuch der Musik-bibliothek Peters* 10 (1904), 17–25.

Plate 1. Anonymous copy (ca. 1730–1750) of the Trio in C Minor, BWV 21/1a (Schwerin, Landesbibliothek Mecklenburg-Vorpommern, *Mus. 888a*. Reproduced with permission.)

sources of Bach's pre-1730 keyboard music. Within the compilation, the Concerto in E♭ Major was copied by Preller, the other pieces by Mempell.[27]

The Trio in C Minor, BWV 585, and the Trio in F Major ("Aria"), BWV 587, are handed down together in an early-nineteenth-century manuscript[28] that probably reflects the now-lost source used to edit volume 9 of the Peters Edition of the complete organ works. In addition to being united in the nineteenth-century manuscript, the two trios share a common origin, since both appear to be derived from materials found in the Dresden court library: the Trio in C Minor is a transcription of the first two movements of Johann Friedrich Fasch's Sonata in C Minor for two violins and continuo, preserved in a set of performance parts in an anonymous hand,[29] and the Trio in F Major is a transcription of the "Air gracieusement" from François Couperin's Trio Sonata in F Major ("La Convalescente"), found in a manuscript score in the hand of Bach's friend and colleague, court concertmaster Johann Georg Pisendel (1687–1755).[30] The two trios may be organ arrangements of "Dresden ditties" that Bach brought home to Leipzig.[31]

Finally, the Trio in D Minor, BWV 583, and Trio in C Minor, BWV 585, are transmitted in sources stemming from the estate of Johann Christian Westphal (1773–1828),[32]

27. Peter Krause, *Handschriften der Werke Johann Sebastian Bachs in der Musikbibliothek der Stadt Leipzig* (Leipzig: Bibliographische Veröffentlichungen der Musikbibliothek der Stadt Leipzig, 1964), 29–36. Andrew Talle, in *J. S. Bach's Keyboard Partitas and Their Early Audience* (PhD diss., Harvard University, 2003), 173–75, has shown that BWV 527/1a, 585, 586, and 1039/4a were written by Mempell rather than by an anonymous assistant, as proposed by Krause.

28. Lüneburg, Ratsbücherei, *Mus. ant. pract. 44*, a ca. 1820 manuscript once owned by W. Wiedemann of Beverstedt. See NBA IV/8, KB, 94.

29. Dresden, Sächsische Landesbibliothek—Staats- und Universitätsbibliothek Dresden, *Mus. 2423-Q-10*. See Hans-Joachim Schulze, "Das c-Moll-Trio BWV 585—eine Orgeltranscription Johann Sebastian Bachs?" in *Deutsches Jahrbuch der Musikwissenschaft* 16 (1973), 150–55.

30. Dresden, Sächsische Landesbibliothek—Staats- und Universitätsbibliothek Dresden, *Mus. 2162-Q-2*. See Delang, "Couperin—Pisendel—Bach," 197–204. Delang demonstrates that the Trio in F Major is derived from an early manuscript version of Couperin's Sonata "La Convalescente" contained in Pisendel's copy, rather than the later printed version of the Sonata "L'impériale" from *Les Nations* of 1726, as previously thought.

31. Forkel reported that J. S. Bach generally took Wilhelm Friedemann on his trips to Dresden in the years before Friedemann secured a position there, and that a few days before his departure Sebastian would say, in jest, "Friedemann, shan't we go again to hear the lovely Dresden ditties?" Forkel, *Über Johann Sebastian Bachs Leben*, 86; NBR, 461.

32. SBB-PK *Mus. ms. Bach P 286*, and *Mus. ms. Bach P 289*, respectively. *P 286* is in an anonymous hand (not that of "Anonymous 300," a Berlin copyist of C. P. E. Bach's from ca. 1755 to the end of the 1760s, as claimed by Paul Kast in *Die Bach-Handschriften der Berliner Staatsbibliothek* [Trossingen: Hohner Verlag, 1958], 20, according to Peter Wollny); *P 289* is in the hand of Westphal.

who studied with Johann Christian Kittel, a Bach student, and C. F. G. Schwencke, C. P. E. Bach's successor as Church Music Director in Hamburg. This suggests a common origin for these two trios, perhaps as works studied by Kittel or C. P. E. Bach in lessons with Johann Sebastian.

In addition to these common ties, it is noteworthy that none of the sources of the miscellaneous trios or Six Sonata variants point to an origin before 1725. The earliest manuscripts are those of Johann Gottfried Walther (1684–1748), Johann Tobias Krebs (1690–1762), Johann Caspar Vogler (1696—1763), and Kellner, which date from around 1725 to 1730 or so—that is, the period leading up to the completion of the Six Sonata collection:

Trio in D Minor, BWV 527/1a	Berlin, *P 1089*, Vogler, ca. 1729[33]
	Bethlehem, Vogler, ca. 1729[34]
Trio in A Minor, BWV 529/2a	Leipzig, *Go. S. 306*, J. T. Krebs, 1725–1726[35]
	Berlin, *P 286*, Kellner, after 1727[36]
	Stockholm, Vogler, ca. 1729[37]
	New Haven, *LM 4718*, Walther, after 1729[38]
Sonata in G Major, BWV 1039/1a	Berlin, *P 804*, Kellner, after 1730[39]

Chronologically, the next group of early manuscripts comprises those of Mempell, which date from the 1730s.

The earliest source and source interconnections of the Six Sonata variants and miscellaneous trios can be summarized as follows in table 1.

33. SBB-PK *Mus. ms. Bach P 1089*. Dating from Schulze, "'Das Stück in Goldpapier,'" 32, and NBA IV/7, KB, 51 and 75. Dietrich Kilian, editor of NBA IV/7, believes Vogler's copy of BWV 527/1a may contain corrections in Bach's hand.

34. Bethlehem, Pennsylvania, Lehigh University, University Library, Special Collections, without call number. Dating from Schulze, *Studien zur Bach-Überlieferung*, 68.

35. Leipzig, Städtische Bibliotheken—Musikbibliothek, Sammlung Gorke, *Go. S. 306*. Dating from NBA IV/7, KB, 53.

36. SBB-PK *Mus. ms. Bach P 286*. Dating from Russell Stinson, *The Bach Manuscripts of Johann Peter Kellner and His Circle: A Case Study in Reception History* (Durham, N.C.: Duke University Press, 1990), 24.

37. Stockholm, Stiftelsen Musikkulturens främjande, without call number. Dating from Schulze, "'Das Stück in Goldpapier,'" 32.

38. New Haven, Connecticut, Yale University, Irving S. Gilmore Music Library, *LM 4718*. Dating from Beißwenger, "Zur Chronologie der Notenhandschriften Johann Gottfried Walthers," 29 and 38n47.

39. SBB-PK *Mus. ms. Bach P 804*. Dating from Russell Stinson, "'Ein Sammelband aus Johann Peter Kellners Besitz': Neue Forschungen zur Berliner Bach-Handschrift P 804," *Bach-Jahrbuch* 78 (1992), 52.

Table 1. Six Sonata Variants and Miscellaneous Free Organ Trios: Earliest Sources and Source Interconnections

		Source Interconnections				
Work	*Earliest Source*[1]	*"35 Organ Trios"*	*Körner*	*Ms. 7*	*Lüneburg*	*Westphal*
Six Sonata Variants						
Trio in E-flat Major, BWV 525/1a	*P 597*, before 1768	×				
Trio in D Minor, BWV 527/1a	*P 1089*, ca. 1729			×		
Trio in D Minor, BWV 528/2a	*Go.S. 311/2*, ca. 1760	×	×			
Trio in A Minor, BWV 529/2a	Stockholm, ca. 1729	×				
	P 286, after 1727					
	Go.S. 306, 1725–26					
Miscellaneous Trios: Bach						
Trio in C Minor, BWV 21/1a	Schwerin, 1730–50		×			
Trio in D Minor, BWV 583	*P 286*, ca. 1755–60s	×	×			×
Trio in G Minor, BWV 584	Körner, 1842		×			
Trio in C Minor, BWV 585	*Ms. 7*, ca. 1730–40			×	×	×
Trio in G Major, BWV 586	*Ms. 7*, ca. 1730–40		×	×		
Trio in F Major, BWV 587	Lüneburg, ca. 1820				×	
Miscellaneous Trios: Bach Circle						
Concerto in E-flat Major, BWV 597	*Ms. 7*, ca. 1743–47			×		
Trio in B Minor, BWV 790a	*Ms. 1*		×			
Trio in C Major, BWV 1014/3a	Körner, 1850		×			
Sonata in G Major, BWV 1039a						
Movement 1	*P 804*, after 1730					
Movement 2	*P 288*, 1850-1900					
Movement 4	*Ms. 7*, ca. 1730–40			×		

Note: 1. For details see the KBs of NBA IV/5-6, IV/7, IV/8, and IV/11.

Bach's Leipzig Workshop

If the bulk of the miscellaneous free organ trios does indeed date from approximately 1725 to 1730, then what factors would have led Bach to focus on the genre in Leipzig at that time? First, it was during this period that Bach's organ "studio" expanded considerably, producing a pressing need for pedagogical material not only for his son Wilhelm Friedemann but for other talented organ students as well. Although Bach had taught organ students in Weimar and Cöthen, Leipzig offered far greater opportunities for private keyboard instruction: he could draw from the student populations of the St. Thomas School and University and could also offer boarding accommodations to visiting students in the large attic dormitory of the St. Thomas School building, in which the cantor's apartment was located. In Weimar and Cöthen Bach had approximately a dozen keyboard students; in Leipzig this number rose to more than seventy.[40]

From a pedagogical standpoint, trios were the organ equivalent of Inventions and Sinfonias for keyboard: they offered instruction in the cantabile manner of performance, finger and foot independence, and composition. The improvisation of chorale trios was a common requirement of auditions for organist positions at the time;[41] free trios would have provided appropriate practice in playing in three independent parts. Moreover, the progressive style of the Six Sonatas and miscellaneous trios would have appealed to a younger generation that favored fashionable, *galant* idioms. Bach's uncanny combination of catchy melodies and technical challenge may have been his way of holding his students to the organ, which was soon to lose favor to more expressive instruments and instrumental ensembles. As such, the Six Sonatas represent the logical culmination of the systematic teaching series that Bach assembled in the 1720s: the Inventions and Sinfonias, the French and English Suites, and the Well-Tempered Clavier, book I.

Second, the trio sonatas and sonata movements allowed Bach to take advantage of the changes that were occurring in the Central German organ in the 1720s and 1730s. While the organ builders of North Germany appeared to be stuck in the seventeenth-century Arp Schnitger mold, the builders of central Germany sought to create progressive organs that were forward-looking, experimental, utilitarian, and closely

40. See the list in NBR, 315–17. To the Leipzig students can be added Bernhard Christian Kayer (formerly known as "Anonymous 5"; 1705–1758), Johann Friedrich Schweinitz (1708–1780), and Gottlob Friedrich Türsch (1709–1779).

41. One of the requirements of the audition for the organist post at the Hamburg Cathedral in 1725, for instance, was to improvise a three-part chorale prelude on the hymn "Herr Jesu Christ, du höchstes Gut" on two keyboards and pedal, without doubling the bass and with independent manual parts. See Johann Mattheson, *Grosse General-Baß-Schule* (Hamburg: Johann Christoph Kißners Buchladen, 1731; reprint Hildesheim: G. Olms, 1968), 34.

allied with chamber music.[42] These builders introduced new stops designed to mimic instruments used in chamber ensembles. For instance, in his proposal for the Castle Church in Altenburg, an instrument Bach played in 1739, Tobias Heinrich Gottfried Trost promised that the Viol di gamba would be "specially voiced to sound like the genuine instrument" and the Hautbois would be "a completely special stop—similar to the natural oboe and also capable of being employed usefully in music-making when the natural instrument is not available."[43] A contemporary visitor to the 1723 Joachim Wagner organ in the Garrison Church in Potsdam, an instrument Bach played during his visit with Frederick the Great in 1747, stated similarly that the Flûte traversière sounded "quite like a real transverse flute, especially in the middle octaves." [44] The result was an organ with stops oriented toward a chamber ensemble, an instrument perfectly suited to trio transcriptions and trio compositions.

Third, the trio sonata as a genre exemplified perfectly the instrumental principles that Bach espoused in Cöthen, where as Capellmeister to the court of Prince Leopold he composed and performed large amounts of chamber music. We can assume trio sonatas played a vital role in the Cöthen repertoire, especially when Prince Leopold traveled to Carlsbad in the summers of 1717, 1718, and 1720, taking with him a reduced retinue of players to provide musical entertainment.[45] By contrast, there is no concrete evidence of this type of activity in Weimar. In Leipzig the trio sonata proved an ideal texture for organ transcriptions, since it transferred to the instrument more easily than the Italian concerto. The trio sonata did not involve the extensive rewriting normally required of concerto arrangements: its harmonic bass could be played comfortably on the pedals, and its two treble voices could be assigned practically without change to separate keyboards. Once transcribed, it served as ideal service, concert, and pedagogical material. In Weimar, Bach arranged concertos in friendly competition with Johann Gottfried Walther. In Leipzig, he seems to have arranged trio sonata movements from his own music as well as that of his contemporaries in friendly competition with colleagues and students. The transcriptions closely follow their originals: other than rewritten pedal lines to bring them into the range of the

42. See Lynn Edwards, "The Thuringian Organ 1702–1720: '. . . ein wohlgerathenes gravitätisches Werk,'" in *The Organ Yearbook* 22 (1991), 119–50; and George B. Stauffer, "Bach's Late Works and the Central German Organ," *Keyboard Perspectives 3* (2011), 115–20.

43. Hans Löffler, "Gottfried Heinrich Trost und die Altenburger Schloßorgel," *Musik und Kirche* 4 (1932), 174.

44. Johann Friedrich Walther, *Die in der königl. Garnisonkirche zu Berlin befindliche neue Orgel* (Berlin, 1727).

45. See Maria Hübner, "Neues zu Johann Sebastian Bachs Reisen nach Karlsbad," *Bach-Jahrbuch* 92 (2006), 93–107.

organ pedalboard, little adjustment was needed. The original organ trios mirror the style of contemporary chamber music, utilizing freely invented *galant* melodic material and da capo, ritornello, ABA, and other balanced designs.

Bach's interest in the organ as a chamber instrument during his first decade in Leipzig is also evident in the sudden appearance of obbligato organ parts in the works of his third annual cantata cycle, compiled between 1725 and 1727. From May to November 1726 Bach suddenly wrote six cantatas containing seventeen movements with organ obbligato, including the bulk of the well-known sinfonias and arias with solo organ.[46] Christoph Wolff has proposed (in this volume) that Bach unveiled this new type of piece, the organ concerto, in his public recital in St. Sophia's Church in Dresden in September 1725.[47] Bach's exploration of this particular idiom may have been spurred by collaborations with his Gotha colleague Gottfried Heinrich Stölzel (1690–1749), who also began writing cantatas with obbligato organ in the second half of the 1720s.[48]

Whatever the case, by 1729 Bach had composed seven more obbligato organ movements, forming a sizable repertory of twenty-four highly idiosyncratic pieces featuring solo organ. In these innovative works Bach brought the organ up to date in a host of pieces displaying dance meters, trio and quartet textures, and progressive idioms. In a number of arias in particular, the musical style mirrors perfectly that of the Six Sonatas and miscellaneous trios. The cantata movements and free organ trios appear to reflect the same compositional aesthetic and seem to be products of the same period.

With these factors in mind, we can at last turn to the miscellaneous trios themselves.

TRIO IN C MINOR, BWV 585. This trio is a transcription of the first two movements of Johann Friedrich Fasch's four-movement "Trio a 2 Violini e Basso." The arrangement is ascribed to Bach in both the Mempell and Westphal manuscripts, and musical refinements in the text—such as improved readings and rhythmic sharpening—point to his direct involvement. A second version of the arrangement attributed to Johann Ludwig Krebs (1713–1780)[49] follows the original sonata text more closely and may be Krebs's response to a transcription assignment from his teacher. Bach may

46. See George B. Stauffer, "Bach's Cantata and Passion Movements with Obbligato Organ," in *Festschrift Ewald Kooiman*, edited by Hans Fidom, Jan R. Luth, and Christoph Wolff (Veenhuizen, Neth.: Boejenga Music, 2008), 19–41.

47. Christoph Wolff, "Did J. S. Bach Write Organ Concertos? Apropos the Prehistory of the Cantata Movements with Obbligato Organ," this volume, 60–75.

48. Matthew Cron, *The Obbligato Organ Cantatas of J. S. Bach in the Context of 18th-Century Practice* (PhD diss., Brandeis University, 2003), 14–38.

49. First published in *Gesammt Ausgabe der Tonstück für die Orgel von John. Ludw. Krebs*, edited by Carl Geissler (Magdeburg: Heinrichshofen, ca. 1848). See NBA IV/8, KB, 85.

have required his organ students to transcribe and then perform especially attractive trio sonata movements as part of instruction. In the case of Fasch's work, the themes (expressive in the first movement, sprightly in the second), harmonic continuo bass, invertible counterpoint of the upper parts, and periodic cadences of the harmonic plan are similar to the style of the Six Sonatas, making this arrangement an ideal study piece for the later, more arduous works.

TRIO IN G MAJOR, BWV 586. Assigned to Bach in the Mempell manuscript and Körner edition, this piece appears to be a transcription of an unidentified trio-sonata movement by a contemporary composer. The *galant* writing with sweet-sounding parallel thirds, the playful turn to minor mode toward the end of each half, and the dance-like meter and binary form suggest that the original was the last movement of a trio sonata, perhaps a work for two flutes and continuo by Telemann.[50] The dance idiom and binary form anticipate the last movement of Sonata 1 in E♭ Major from the Six Sonatas.

TRIO IN F MAJOR ("ARIA"), BWV 587. The recent discovery of the Couperin trio-sonata model for this work in Pisendel's manuscript at the Dresden court tightens the connection of the Trio in F Major with Bach.[51] Two small changes in the text also suggest Bach's handiwork: the correction of the rhythmic notation of the trill and turn in the main theme (dotted 16th and two 32nds in Pisendel's score; dotted 16th and two 64ths in the transcription) and the rhythmic sharpening at the cadence in m. 39 (8th and two 16ths in Pisendel's score; dotted 8th and two 32nds in the transcription). The fully obbligato pedal part, which includes trills, and the well-designed ABA form show a kindred spirit with the first movement of Sonata 3 in D Minor of the Six Sonatas.

Pointing directly to Bach's workshop are transcriptions of his own works, which often rely on versions that are no longer extant.

TRIO IN C MINOR, BWV 21/1a. The recent discovery of the Schwerin manuscript raises the possibility that this transcription, derived from a ca. 1720 version of the Sinfonia from Cantata 21, stems from Bach. Like the Trio in G Minor, BWV 584, the Trio in C Minor is a distillation of its model, produced by drawing on the oboe, violin 1, and continuo parts of the sinfonia while dropping the remaining string lines. The left-hand part, derived from violin 1 of the sinfonia, nevertheless borrows from the viola at one point, just as the left-hand part of the G-Minor Trio, based on violin 1 of its aria model, borrows from the tenor line here and there. Thus from a procedural

50. Karl Anton, in *Musik und Kirche* 1942/2, 47–49, claimed that the G-Major Trio is based on a harpsichord piece (perhaps a transcription?) by Telemann contained in a manuscript volume dating from Telemann's years in Leipzig (1701–1705). The volume was destroyed in World War II, before Anton could publish his findings.

51. See note 30.

point of view, the two trios are closely related. As we have noted, the C-Minor Trio is paired with the Six Sonatas in the Schwerin manuscript. Also tying it to the Six Sonatas is its style: the expressive cantilena melodies, the 8th-note walking bass, and the invertible counterpoint of the treble lines mirror the minor-key slow movements of Sonata 1 in E♭ Major, Sonata 5 in C Major, and Sonata 6 in G Major, in particular. The dramatic pauses leading to the final measures mark the sinfonia as one of Bach's most expressive Weimar instrumental creations. It's hardly surprising that Bach decided to recycle the music in Leipzig as an organ trio.

TRIO IN G MINOR, BWV 584. There are reasons to believe that this trio transcription, too, stems from Bach himself or his immediate milieu. The arranger had access to the original score or a complete set of performance parts for Cantata 166. In addition, he synthesized the violin and tenor parts to produce a single, composite left-hand line—a distillation process requiring considerable artistry. The transcriber also used only the A section of the aria model, a "torso" technique employed by Bach in the B-Minor Mass and other parody works. Finally, the arranger created a new, wordless syncopated version of the principal theme by tying beats 3 and 4 of the first measure (example 1). In the middle of the trio, the tie is dropped to produce development-like activity. Who but Bach would have made these changes to produce such a compelling organ trio?

TRIO IN B MINOR, BWV 790a. This transcription of the Sinfonia 4 in D Minor, BWV 790, is handed down in a manuscript attributed to Leonhard Frischmuth (d. 1764), dated ca.1740–1760,[52] and in Körner's *Sammtliche Orgel-Compositionen von Joh. Sebastian Bach*. Frischmuth studied with Kellner, who had access to Bach manuscripts in the 1720s and 1730s and was involved with organ trio transcriptions of various works, to judge from his copy of the Trio in G Major, BWV 1039/1a (see below). The sinfonia text has been transposed down a third, from D minor to B minor, to bring the bass line into a more suitable range for an organ pedalboard with the compass C—d′. Both Frischmuth and Kellner have been proposed as possible transcribers,[53] while two small improvements hint at Bach's possible supervision: the trill in m. 2 (absent in the original) nicely embellishes the cadential figure in the right hand, and the d′ in the pedal in m. 17 (an octave higher than the original) improves the melodic contour of the bass line. But the lack of any substantive changes in the musical text points to a product from Bach's circle rather than an arrangement by the composer himself.

52. Leipzig, Städtische Bibliotheken—Musikbibliothek, *Ms. 1*. Dating from Russell Stinson, *The Manuscripts of Johann Peter Kellner and His Circle* (Durham, N.C.: Duke University Press, 1989), 38–40, and NBA IV/11, KB, 160–61.

53. Stinson, *The Bach Manuscripts of Johann Peter Kellner*, 79, and NBA IV/11, KB, 161.

Ex. 1a. Cantata 166, Aria "Ich will an den Himmel denken," oboe, mm. 1–3

Ex. 1b. Trio in G minor, BWV 584, mm. 1–3

TRIO IN C MAJOR, BWV 1014/3a. This transcription of the third movement of the Sonata 1 in B Minor for Violin and Harpsichord, BWV 1014, is transmitted solely in Körner's *Sammtliche Orgel-Compositionen*. The music has been transposed from D major to C major and small changes have been made here and there to accommodate the range of a C—c´´ keyboard and C—c´ pedalboard. A variant reading in the left hand part (in m. 15) suggests that the trio may have been derived from a now-lost alternate version of the violin and harpsichord sonata.[54] All performance indications in the instrumental score—tempo marking, ornaments, and slurs—are absent in the organ trio. Though this aspect of the arrangement—along with its transposition to accommodate keyboard range and various small alterations in the text—is characteristic of transcriptions from Bach's workshop, the lack of any significant improvements to the text suggests once again an arranger other than Bach himself.

SONATA IN G MAJOR, BWV 1039/1a, 2a, and 4a. Three movements from the Sonata in G Major for Two Flutes and Continuo, BWV 1039, or its model are passed down as independent transcriptions: movement 1 in a manuscript written by Kellner after 1730,[55] movement 2 in an anonymous manuscript from the second half of the eighteenth century,[56] and movement 4 in the Mempell manuscript from ca.1730–1740.[57] Russell Stinson, who has analyzed the three arrangements in detail, concludes that the first two show procedural similarities (transposition of the left-hand part down an octave, alteration of the bass line to fit the compass of a C—c´ pedalboard) and

54. See NBA IV/11, KB, 162.

55. SBB-PK *Mus. Ms. Bach P 804*. Dating from Stinson, *The Manuscripts of Johann Peter Kellner and His Circle*, 62.

56. SBB-PK *Mus. Ms. Bach P 288*. Dating from NBA IV/5–6, KB, 60.

57. Leipzig, Städtische Bibliotheken—Musikbibliothek, Sammlung Mempell-Preller, *Ms. 7*. Dating from Schulze, "Wie enstand die Bach-Sammlung Mempell-Preller?" 120.

may represent Kellner's handiwork.[58] Kelner's copy of movement 1 ends with "Sequi allegro"' the arrangement of movement 2 may be this sequel. The transcription of movement 4 is more complicated, with treble lines reversed here and there and continuo material transferred to the left hand at two spots to produce hybrid statements of the theme. In addition, seven measures from the original have been dropped. The result is a corrupt yet highly effective transcription, probably by someone other than the arranger of movements 1 and 2. Taken as a whole, the three trios seem to reflect transcription projects within Bach's workshop.

CONCERTO IN E♭ MAJOR, BWV 597. This arrangement, apparently the outer movements of a three-movement "Sonate auf Concertenart" (sonata in the manner of a concerto), surfaced only in 1904 with the first report of the Mempell-Preller Collection. Bearing the title "Concerto in Dis-dur à 2 Clavier con Pedale di Mons: Bach" in the Preller manuscript, it was included for a while in the Peters Edition of the Bach organ works but was subsequently dropped.[59] The pedal solo that serves as a bridge between the two principal sections of movement 1 (mm. 25–28) hints at an original work for organ. The unabashedly *galant* qualities of the first movement and the inconsistent part writing of the Gigue point beyond Bach to a composer of a younger generation, perhaps one of Bach's sons (a fifteen-year-old Wilhelm Friedemann) or students (Heinrich Nicolaus Gerber, who published a now-lost set of *Concert-Trios* in 1734).[60] The attribution to "Mons. Bach" suggests a tie with the Bach circle, and certain aspects of the music reflect concerto qualities found in the Six Sonatas: the unison opening of movement 1 (= movement 1, Sonata 6)[61] and the imitative binary form of the Gigue (= movement 3, Sonata 1), for instance (example 2). Although seldom performed today, the Concerto in E♭ Major is a meritorious piece that sheds important light on progressive stylistic currents under consideration in Bach's circle in Leipzig.

TRIO IN D MINOR, BWV 583, also appears to be an original organ work rather than a transcription of an instrumental trio sonata movement. It is attributed to Bach

58. Russell Stinson, "Three Organ-Trio Transcriptions from the Bach Circle: Keys to a Lost Bach Chamber Work," in *Bach Studies*, edited by Don Franklin (Cambridge: Cambridge University Press, 1989), 125–59.

59. It was published in the first revised version of volume 9 (2nd ed., edited by Max Seiffert, 1904) but removed from the second revised version of the same volume (3rd ed., edited by Hermann Keller, 1940).

60. The latter edition is listed in the *Historisch-biographisches Lexicon der Tonkünstler* (1790) of Gerber's son Ernst Ludwig.

61. The unison opening, indicated by music's notation, has frequently been misinterpreted by modern editors. See *Johann Sebastian Bach: The Complete Organ Works*, edited by George B. Stauffer, vol. 7 (Leupold, 2014), 149, note for mm. 1–3.

Ex. 2. Concerto in E♭ Major, BWV 597/1 and 3, mm. 1–5

consistently in the sources—a manuscript from the Westphal estate, the two "35 Orgeltrios" fragments, and a Körner edition—and its style is characteristic of his writing. The Trio's idiomatic organ figuration (mm. 24–25 and mm. 35–36, especially), ABA form, imitative treatment, and high degree of thematic integration (with blocks of repeated material either transposed or with treble parts reversed, or both) are typical of the middle movements of the Six Sonatas. Indeed, the piece's structure is built on the same principles as the *Adagio e dolce* of Sonata 3 in D Minor:

Section	*Mm.*	*Material*	*Description*	*Key*
A	1–7	a1	imitative theme	i
	7–13	a2	imitative sequences, derived from a1	III
	13–19	a1	treble parts reversed	i
B	19–24	b1	imitative theme derived from a2	VI
	24–25	b2	imitative theme derived from a2	
	26–27	b3	imitative theme derived from a2	
	28–29	b3	treble parts reversed, bass elaborated	
	30–35	b1	transposed, treble parts reversed	iv
	35–36	b2	transposed, treble parts reversed	
	37–38	b3	transposed, treble parts reversed	
	39–40	b3	transposed, treble parts reversed, bass elaborated	
A´	41–45	a1	transposed	(i)
	45–50	a2	transposed, treble parts reversed	VI
	51–53	a	coda	i

Both the nature of the music and its modern D-minor notation speak to a post-Weimar origin.[62] One wonders, in fact, whether the Trio in D Minor might not be a discarded Trio Sonata movement, sketched in the same workbook as the surviving Trio Sonata variants but not used. Its transmission in the "35 Organ Trios" with three of the four Trio Sonata variant movements strengthens this conjecture. The piece's transmission with the sonata variants also suggests a composition date of ca. 1725–1729, the period during which Bach was assembling the Trio Sonatas. The D-Minor Trio is also handed down in a highly embellished version, suggesting that Bach may have used it subsequently in organ instruction, perhaps with an ornament-happy student such as Heinrich Nicolaus Gerber or Bernhard Christian Kayser.[63]

Summary

One can propose, then, that the miscellaneous organ trios and Six Sonata variants represent a unified repertory springing from a single period of activity in Leipzig: 1725 to 1730 or so. They served as preparatory exercises for the Six Sonatas, as display pieces

62. D minor with one flat, as opposed to "Dorian" notation with no flats, which Bach abandoned around 1720.

63. The ornamented version was printed in volume 4 the Peters Edition by Friedrich Conrad Griepenkerl, who worked from two now-lost manuscript copies of the trio. Gerber's and Kayser's ornamented versions of several three-part sinfonias are printed in NBA V/3, Anhang I and Anhang II.

for demonstrating the chamber-music registers of the progressive Central German organ, and as teaching material for students such as Gerber, Johann Tobias Krebs, Johann Ludwig Krebs, and Gottfried August Homilius (1714–1785), who went on to compose trio sonatas of their own. If this hypothesis is correct, the completion of the Six Sonatas around 1730 emerges not as a sudden, isolated event, but rather as the logical outcome of a period of concentrated study and experimentation with the free organ trio. That Bach may have drafted material for the Six Sonatas in a workbook is implied by the common transmission of three Sonata variants and the Trio in D Minor, BWV 583. The existence of such a workbook would help to explain the fair-copy appearance of the Six Sonatas in Bach's autograph manuscript, *P 271*, which is clearly based on pre-existing drafts or sketches.[64]

The above systematic review of the miscellaneous trios also lends a new perspective on the pieces themselves—suggesting, for example, that the Trio in C Minor, BWV 21/1a, and Trio in G Minor, BWV 584, are products of Bach's pen and merit placement in the composer's canon of established works. It also raises the likelihood that the Concerto in E♭ Major, BWV 597; Trio in B Minor, BWV 790a; Trio in C Major, BWV 1014/3a; and Sonata in G Major, BWV 1039a, were created in Bach's workshop, by his colleagues and students. Although the miscellaneous trios "do not equal" the Six Sonatas, as Forkel pointed out two centuries ago, they may nevertheless "be reckoned fine" and worthy of consideration and performance today.

64. See especially John Butt, "Bach's Organ Sonatas BWV 525–530: Compilation and Recomposition," in *The Organ Yearbook* 19 (1988), 80–90.

Did J. S. Bach Write Organ Concertos?

Apropos the Prehistory of Cantata Movements with Obbligato Organ

Christoph Wolff

Johann Sebastian Bach's third Leipzig cantata cycle, begun on the first Sunday after Trinity in 1725 and spread over more than two years, contains no fewer than four cantatas with extended opening concerto movements that feature virtuoso organ solo parts. One additional such concerto-sinfonia follows in a later cantata from the so-called Picander cycle of 1728. That a composer could lay claim to the liturgy of the Lutheran worship service and turn the church at least momentarily into a concert hall is an extraordinary phenomenon, one without precedent in the history of the church cantata. Although the use of the obbligato organ in church cantatas was by no means new (Bach himself introduced an organ solo in the first aria of his 1708 Mühlhausen cantata BWV 71), a full-scale concerto movement as a cantata opening was definitely a novelty; it took up, after all, a substantial portion of the service. In the case of BWV 146, for example, no less than seven and a half minutes of virtuosic instrumental music are heard before the first words sung by the choir identify the cantata as a piece of sacred music.

Concerto-style sinfonias featuring a virtuoso performer with extensive solo passages, cadenzas, and the like differ conceptually from ordinary and typically concise instrumental introductions to cantata choruses. The former kind of movement shifts the focus from musically enhanced biblical messages and spiritual reflections to an ostentatious instrumental presentation, thereby altering the functionality of the cantata as a musical sermon. A more effective demonstration of Bach's self-confidence and self-esteem is hard to imagine. In just a few years he had managed to carve out for himself a commanding position in Leipzig, and in the realm of church music he clearly held his own vis-à-vis the Lutheran clergy. If the consistory had considered such concerto extravaganzas in church services an unwelcome distraction, it could easily have stopped the cantor from mounting such pieces. Curiously, however, nothing at all is known about any such action. On the contrary, since Bach presented cantatas with concertato organ sinfonias not only once but several times between 1725 and 1728—and indeed, by way of repeat performances, throughout his Leipzig tenure—this can only mean that neither the clergy, the congregation, nor anyone else objected to this innovative type of church music. They may, in fact, have thoroughly enjoyed it.

Table 1 presents an overview of the five pertinent cantatas and their concerto-sinfonias. Not included is the organ sinfonia from BWV 29, a clever arrangement of the *Preludio* from the unaccompanied violin partita in E major (BWV 1006/1), because it is not strictly speaking a concerto movement. It constitutes, nevertheless, an instrumental movement with a virtuosic solo part, which served in 1729 as the opening for the second part of the wedding cantata *Herr Gott, Beherrscher aller Dinge*, BWV 120a. In 1731 Bach reused this movement as a sinfonia for the town council election cantata *Wir danken dir, Gott*, BWV 29. Also omitted from table 1 are the slow concerto movements that were converted into arias in such works as BWV 146, 35, and 169. For the purpose of this essay, which explores the prehistory of the cantata movements with obbligato organ, the sinfonias of Cantatas 146 and 169 will form the center of the discussion. Before going into details about these works, however, a few general remarks seem in order.

It may not be a coincidence that one of the cantatas, perhaps the first composed of the group, was performed on Jubilate Sunday—in other words, the traditional opening Sunday for the spring trade fair, which regularly brought to Leipzig a mass of outside visitors and many representatives of the European nobility. BWV 146 cannot be exactly dated to either 1726 or 1727, so performances in either or perhaps even both years are possible. In 1727, for example, Saxon Elector and Polish King Friedrich August I attended the spring fair with his large entourage; a few days after Jubilate Sunday, on May 12, 1727, Bach presented a festive and lavish open-air *Abend-Music* in his honor (BWV Anh. 9—music lost). The town chronicler refers to the participation of forty

Table 1. Concerto movements with obbligato organ

May 12, 1726 (Jubilate Sunday) or 1727	*Wir müssen durch viel Trübsal*, BWV 146
	1. Sinfonia in d
September 8, 1726 (12th Sunday after Trinity)	*Geist und Seele wird verwirret*, BWV 35
	1. Sinfonia in d
	5. Sinfonia in d
October 20, 1726 (18th Sunday after Trinity)	*Gott soll allein mein Herze haben*, BWV 169
	1. Sinfonia in D
November 3, 1726 (20th Sunday after Trinity)	*Ich geh und suche mit Verlangen*, BWV 49
	1. Sinfonia in E

musicians and the presence of three hundred university students whose torches lit the outdoor performance site on the market square.[1]

At both St. Nicholas Church and St. Thomas Church, Bach used large church organs as part of the continuo group for his cantatas. These same instruments served, of course, for the solo roles in the concerto sinfonias as well. Because the organs were tuned in choir pitch, a whole tone above chamber pitch, the figured organ continuo parts as well as the organ solo parts had to be transposed down. This meant, for example, that the solo parts for the D-minor sinfonia of BWV 146 as well as the D-major sinfonia were notated in C minor and C major, respectively. This fact made for optimal use of the traditional four-octave compass *C* to *c´´´* of the manual keyboards and similarly of the shorter range (*Contra C* to *d*) of the pedal keyboard.[2] The key choice of C minor and C major implied at the same time the pointed and effective use of the organ's largest pipes, which would emphasize the instrument's gravitas. Pedal use for certain exposed passages in the organ solo part must also be assumed even though not specifically indicated, since the organ part's bass line runs parallel to the continuo part. A 16´ for the left-hand part may further enhance the continuo fundament of the score.

The extant original performing parts of the sinfonias do not include separate organ solo parts. This suggests that the soloist played directly from the score, whose organ part, notated in choir pitch,[3] left much room for improvisatory additions by the player—in all likelihood Johann Sebastian Bach himself. Although concrete information on this particular point is lacking, most everything speaks for the composer as organ soloist.[4] Bach then would have left the conducting to his principal assistant, the first choir prefect.

Bach's cantata sinfonias with obbligato organ show a particularly close relationship to two of his harpsichord concertos from the collection the composer assembled around 1738.[5] The autograph volume (SBB-PK *Mus. ms. Bach* P 234) comprises seven harpsichord concertos:

1. BDOK II, nos. 219–20.

2. For details regarding the Leipzig organs, see OBH, 50–54.

3. Only four autograph scores of cantatas with concerto movements for obbligato organ have survived: the fragmentary score of BWV 188/1 notates the organ solo part in choir pitch (C minor) and all other instrumental and vocal parts in chamber pitch (D minor); likewise, the score of cantatas BWV 35/1 and 5, BWV 49/1, and BWV 169/1 and 5, respectively, have only the solo parts notated in choir pitch.

4. See the discussion by Laurence Dreyfus, "The Metaphorical Soloist: Concerted Organ Parts in Bach's Cantatas," *Early Music* 13 (1985): 237–47.

5. For a description of the autograph score and its dating, see Werner Breig, NBA VII/4 (2001), KB, 15–21.

D minor, BWV 1052
E major, BWV 1053
D major, BWV 1054
A major, BWV 1055
F minor, BWV 1056
F major, BWV 1057
G minor, BWV 1058

It also contains the beginning of an eighth concerto in D minor (BWV 1059), the score of which, however, breaks off after only nine measures.

Table 2 shows how the various movements of four cantatas (BWV 49, 146, 169, and 188) from the later 1720s were recycled in three works that appear some ten years later as harpsichord concertos in P 234. BWV 1052 and 1053, which open the autograph score, share two movements each with two cantatas: BWV 146 and 169. BWV 35—the only cantata that seems to have integrated an entire three-movement concerto—lacks its full parallel harpsichord concerto version in P 234; only the beginning of BWV 1059/1 is notated. However, the first two harpsichord concertos in P 234, by way of their corresponding cantata sinfonias, provide an informative glimpse at the prehistory of these concerted movements.

The harpsichord concerto in E major (BWV 1053) and its three corresponding cantata movements with obbligato organ (BWV 169/1, 5 and 49/1) present a particularly revealing case. Many questions have been raised about their possible common origin in a three-movement concerto for solo instrument and strings. However, the most important question regarding the identity of the original solo instrument remains unanswered. Werner Breig, editor of these concertos for the *Neue Bach-Ausgabe*, left

Table 2. Cantata sinfonias and harpsichord concertos

	1. Concerto in d, BWV 1052
Sinfonia in d, BWV 146/1	Allegro
Chorus BWV 146/2	Adagio
Sinfonia in d, BWV 188/1	Allegro
	2. Concerto in E, BWV 1053
Sinfonia in D, BWV 169/1	[Allegro]
Aria BWV 169/5	Siciliano
Sinfonia in E, BWV 49/1	Allegro
	7. Concerto fragment in d, BWV 1059
Sinfonia in d, BWV 35/1	[Allegro] – breaks off in m. 9.
Aria BWV 35/2	[Siciliano]
Sinfonia in d, BWV 35/5	[Allegro]

open the question of the original solo instrument for BWV 1053, stating cautiously that the lost first version of the concerto suggests having been written "for a concertato melody instrument." He adds that "the question concerning its solo instrument and key has not found a generally accepted answer." Nevertheless, despite problems surrounding the identity of the original solo instrument, there circulate today several modern reconstructions of this concerto, with the solo part assigned variously to oboe (in F or E-flat major), oboe d'amore (in D major), flute (in F major), and viola (in E-flat major).[6]

Breig's caution over the original solo instrument and key is well founded, for none of the reconstructions mentioned above is truly plausible. Regular oboe, oboe d'amore, and transverse flute are most frequently considered for the solo part, but the unusually extended, indeed virtually endless chains of uninterrupted sixteenth notes and triplet sixteenths in the finale movement BWV 1053/3 (for example, mm. 17–32, 49–64, 81–96, and so on) leave absolutely no room for breathing; as a whole, the movement lacks idiomatic woodwind writing. A solo viola, on the other hand, can realize effectively the perpetual passagework, yet the complete absence of typical string figuration speaks against this instrument. Surprisingly, the possibility that Bach may have originally conceived and intended the solo part for keyboard has apparently never been seriously considered.[7]

The same pertains to the D-minor concerto, BWV 1052. For nearly 150 years, this piece has been considered an arrangement by Bach of an original violin concerto, written either by himself or by another composer.[8] Wilhelm Rust, editor-in-chief of the *Bachgesellschaft* edition and also editor of the concerto volume 17/3 (1869), boldly hypothesized in his introduction that since three of the seven concertos (BWV 1054,

6. Breig (NBA VII/4 [2001], KB, 15–21) discusses attempts at reconstruction as a concerto for transverse flute by Ulrich Siegele; for oboe in E-flat by Ulrich Siegele, Wilfried Fischer, and Joshua Rifkin; for oboe d'amore in D Major by Arnold Mehl and Bruce Haynes; for viola in E-flat by Wilfried Fischer.

7. See, however, my suggestion of the possibility of a solo keyboard instrument in *Johann Sebastian Bach: The Learned Musician* (New York: Norton, 2000), 318, and in "Sicilianos and Organ Recitals: Observations on J. S. Bach's Concertos," in *Bach Perspectives 7: J. S. Bach's Concerted Ensemble Music: The Concerto*, edited by Gregory Butler (Urbana: University of Illinois Press, 2008), 111. See also in this volume the essay by Gregory Butler, "The Choir Loft as Chamber," which considers specifically the harpsichord as original solo instrument.

8. Ulrich Siegele, *Kompositionsweise und Bearbeitungstechnik in der Instrumentalmusik Johann Sebastian Bachs* (Neuhausen-Stuttgart: Hänssler, 1975), 109–11, raised questions about the authenticity of the model for BWV 1052 as an original work by J. S. Bach. These questions were more fully explored by Werner Breig, "Bachs Violinkonzert d-Moll: Studien zu seiner Gestalt und seiner Entstehungsgeschichte," *Bach-Jahrbuch* 62 (1976), 7–34, and Ralph Lewis, "Zur Frage der Authentizität von Bachs Violinkonzert d-Moll," *Bach-Jahrbuch* 65 (1979), 19–28.

1057, and 1058) had extant original models in which violin was the solo instrument, all of Bach's harpsichord concertos were in fact transcriptions of concertos for solo violin. Philipp Spitta and subsequent Bach scholars generally shared this view:[9] the first edition of the *Bach-Werke-Verzeichnis* (1950) states plainly that "with the exception of the second, all concertos are based on violin concertos."[10] BWV 1053 was considered an early exception, soon joined by BWV 1055 and 1056 as works written for a solo wind or at least an instrument other than the violin.[11] However, the status of the D-minor concerto, BWV 1052, as an original violin concerto was never called into question. On the contrary, the reconstructed D-minor violin concerto made it into the NBA,[12] further improvements to its text were suggested by Breig,[13] and ever since the piece has been widely accepted as an authentic Bach violin concerto. Violinists play it occasionally even though, on both technical and musical levels, the piece bears little resemblance to Bach's genuine violin concertos in A minor and E major or to the double violin concerto, BWV 1043. But to return to the matter at hand: What speaks against the D-minor concerto as an original keyboard concerto? After all, in close analogy to the E-major concerto, BWV 1053, and unlike all other harpsichord concertos, its compositional prehistory includes a complete set of cantata movements with obbligato organ. This raises the question for both BWV 1052 and 1053: Did Bach initially write organ concertos, which eventually made it into cantata movements from the third Leipzig *Jahrgang*?

There is in fact documentary evidence for organ concertos played by Bach in prior years. A 1725 newspaper report describes two recitals given on the new Silbermann organ in St. Sophia Church in Dresden:

> Dresden, 21 September 1725.
>
> When the Capell-Director from Leipzig, Mr. Bach, came here recently, he was very well received by the local virtuosos at court and in the city, since he is greatly admired by all of them for his musical adroitness and art. Yesterday and the day before, in the presence of the same, he performed for over an hour on the new organ in St. Sophia's Church preludes and various concertos, with supporting soft instrumental music (*mit unterlauffender Doucen Instrumental-Music*) in all keys.[14]

The specific reference to "diverse concertos with supporting [accompanying] soft instrumental music" can refer only to concertos for solo organ with strings. The ac-

9. Philipp Spitta, *Johann Sebastian Bach* (Leipzig: Breitkopf and Härtel, 1873–1880), II, 618+.

10. BWV[1], 586: "Bis auf das zweite gehen sämtliche Konzerte auf Violinkonzerte zurück."

11. See Breig, NBA VII/4, KB, 132–33 and 158–59.

12. NBA VII/7 (supplement), edited by Wilfried Fischer.

13. NBA VII/4, KB, 15–21.

14. BDOK II, no. 191.

companying ensemble of freelancing court and town musicians was probably led by Johann Georg Pisendel, whom Bach had known for about twenty years and who in 1717 had arranged for the keyboard competition with Louis Marchand. The phrase "in all keys" must not be taken literally, for playing preludes and concertos in all twenty-four keys could hardly be accomplished in two recitals, even when each lasted "over an hour." The reference does suggest, however, that Bach played in various keys, including some remote ones, in order to demonstrate the capabilities of the new instrument.[15]

What kind of "diverse concertos" could Bach have played in Dresden on September 19–20, 1725? No concertos for solo organ and string orchestra by Bach have been transmitted. The only such compositions occur in the cantatas from the third Leipzig cycle, but in these works strings are complemented by three oboes. This raises the possibility if not the likelihood that Bach opened his later collection of harpsichord concertos with two works that, from the outset, featured keyboard as the solo instrument. Moreover, since the cantata scores clearly show that the movements with obbligato organ were not newly composed but copied, pre-cantata versions of BWV 1052 and 1053 must definitely have existed in some form by 1726. If indeed their original versions were concertos for keyboard (possibly either organ or harpsichord) and strings, both would be likely candidates for the Dresden programs of September 1725.

The origin of the autograph score P 234 more than a decade after the related cantata scores does not undermine this supposition; it rather suggests that Bach developed the concept of a collection of harpsichord concertos only in the mid- to late 1730s. On the other hand, the extant composing scores for the cantatas with obbligato organ indicate that the combination of organ and orchestra in the form of concerto movements was definitely not invented for this purpose. Unfortunately, the surviving sources do not allow tracking the origins of the keyboard concerto in Bach's oeuvre beyond the special and quite different use of the harpsichord in the Fifth Brandenburg Concerto or beyond the Weimar arrangements of orchestral concertos by Vivaldi and others for solo organ (BWV 592–596) and solo harpsichord (BWV 972–987) from around 1713–1714. Nevertheless, the assumption seems logical that Bach experimented with and composed concertos for keyboard with orchestral accompaniment as court organist in Weimar, where the duke, as the composer's obituary put it, "fired him with the desire to try every possible artistry in his treatment of the organ."[16] Hence, one can hardly go wrong in placing Bach's initial experimentation with the concerto for keyboard and orchestra in his Weimar period.[17]

15. For details regarding the organ, see OBH, 15–16.

16. NBR, 300.

17. This would also provide a logical prehistory for the prominent and dominating function of the harpsichord as one of three solo instruments in the Fifth Brandenburg Concerto, the oldest source

This may have direct implications for the genesis of the D-minor concerto, BWV 1052. The view that the model for BWV 1052 was not composed by Bach is now rejected by most scholars, including Werner Breig.[18] Furthermore, Breig has argued convincingly for a Weimar origin of the putative D-minor violin concerto and for a date sometime after 1714, primarily because of its approach to ritornello form, a certain stylistic incoherence, and aspects of compositional technique that differ from most of Bach's other concertos. To this two additional points might be taken into consideration: first, the prominent unison ritornello themes of the D-minor concerto relate closely to Vivaldi's *L'estro armonico* (1711), a collection Bach encountered and worked with around 1713–14. Second, since a concerto for keyboard and orchestra was a novel idea, the composer could not draw on established models for idiomatic virtuoso passagework. A violinist himself, Bach took typical string passagework and specific violin manners like *bariolage* as points of departure for the development of virtuoso keyboard figuration.

Supporting evidence for the view that the D-minor violin concerto may have been just a phantom is provided by a set of performing parts copied after 1734 by Carl Philipp Emanuel Bach (SBB-PK *Mus. ms. Bach St 350*). This source was long considered to represent an early version of the D-minor harpsichord concerto (BWV 1052a) until Georg von Dadelsen suggested that it represented an independent arrangement by its young copyist, Bach's second son. The NBA accepted this view and published this version as an early work by C. P. E. Bach (BWV 1052a). However, the context and circumstances of the copying job indicate that BWV 1052a, along with other instrumental works by his father, served Carl Philipp Emanuel Bach between 1734 and 1738—that is, before the assembly of P 234, the autograph of all six harpsichord concerti—as repertoire for his Collegium Musicum at Frankfurt/Oder.[19] In other words, the solo part as well as the string parts of BWV 1052a actually represent the earliest extant layer in the traceable history of Johann Sebastian Bach's D-minor concerto. They also point to a stage of the work that precedes the cantata adaptations of 1726.

Table 3 lists the principal manuscripts for the D-minor keyboard concerto in chronological order according to the proposed compositional history. "A" designates the earliest known version of the concerto, a copy by C. P. E. Bach most likely taken from the

---

of which dates from about 1719. The idea of a concerto for organ or harpsichord as solo instrument occurred to at least one other virtuoso keyboard player fairly early in the eighteenth century: Handel included a sonata featuring a brilliant organ solo part in his first oratorio *Il trionfo del tempo e del disinganno*, HWV 46a, composed 1707 in Rome.

18. See the pages cited in note 5 above and KB, 52.

19. Peter Wollny, "Zur Überlieferung der Instrumentalwerke Johann Sebastian Bachs: Der Quellenbesitz Carl Philipp Emanuel Bachs," *Bach-Jahrbuch* 82 (1996), 7–21.

Table 3. The principal sources of the D-minor keyboard concerto

A	**Copy of a complete set of parts by C. P. E. Bach: SBB-PK, *Mus. ms. Bach St 350*.** Undated early version of the concerto for keyboard and string accompaniment BWV 1052a; left-hand part undeveloped.
B	**Score copy of cantata BWV 146 by J. F. Agricola: SBB-PK, *Am.B. 538*.** Revised version of concerto movements from 1726-27, adapted for organ (left-hand part undeveloped) and with three oboes added to the strings. Solo part notated in d, indicating "in C moll zu transponiren." No original sources survive for this cantata.
C	**Autograph score of the harpsichord concertos BWV 1052-1059: SBB-PK, *Mus. ms. Bach P 234*.** Second revised version of BWV 1052 from ca. 1738, with left-hand part for harpsichord written out.

original performing parts of his father's keyboard concerto (BWV 1052a), with readings completely independent of any later version. "B" designates the intermediate version for obbligato organ as represented in the cantatas BWV 146 and 188. "C" refers to a thorough revision of A by taking B into consideration, too, and includes a fully developed left-hand harpsichord part. The following examples from the first movement of the concerto illuminate the evolution of the work, in particular its solo part.

The kind of extended and extreme virtuosic passagework that appears in all three versions cannot found in any of Bach's violin concertos (BWV 1041–1043). However, as the origin of the Italian solo concerto is so closely identified with that of the violin concerto, there is no question that the general concept of the D-minor concerto and particularly the design of its virtuosic solo material was shaped significantly by violin technique. It is hardly surprising to note that Bach, who was both a violinist and keyboard player, employed in his keyboard concertos idiomatic solo violin figuration because of the absence of equivalent keyboard models for the development of virtuosic passagework. This helps to explain, for example, how the *bariolage* technique in the D-minor Partita for unaccompanied violin (example 3) provided the prototypical idea for the figurative patterns shown in example 2.

Similarly, Bach's transcriptions of Vivaldi's opus 3 display direct translations of characteristic violin figuration into idiomatic passagework for the keyboard, particularly in the first and last movements of the organ concerto in A minor after Vivaldi (BWV 593). The many traces of formative changes in the harpsichord solo parts of the autograph score P 234, on the other hand, do not reflect the process of transcribing violin parts into harpsichord parts but rather indicate the composer's search for an appropriate harpsichord idiom. They suggest a systematic working out of the right- and left-hand parts in terms of refinement, improvement, and amplification of the "violin style" keyboard figuration of his own earlier keyboard concerti.

Ex. 1. Concerto in D Minor, BWV 1052/1, opening of solo parts in versions A–C, mm. 7–10

Ex. 2. Concerto in D Minor, BWV 1052/1, solo passage-work in versions A–C, mm. 146–48

Ex. 3. *Ciaconna*, BWV 1004/5, mm. 236–37

Another question pertains to the more specific elaboration of the continuo-related left-hand harpsichord parts in P 234. Early keyboard concertos, whether by Bach, Handel, or other composers, all have in common the clear emphasis on the right-hand part and the treble register.[20] The left-hand parts in the cantata movements for obbligato organ are by and large identical with the basso continuo parts. However, the apparent emphasis on the right-hand parts may not point to derivation from a

20. Quite comparable in this respect is Mozart's notation of only the right-hand solo part in the autograph score of his piano concerto, K. 537.

supposed solo part for violin, oboe, or other melody instrument but may rather reflect specific performance conditions. If—as the evidence suggests—the solo organ parts in these movements were indeed played by the composer, he would not have needed a detailed realization of the left-hand part. Bass and treble lines would have been sufficient in defining the scaffolding for the soloist's improvisatory elaboration. Moreover, the choice of stops for the obbligato organ had to be different from ordinary continuo accompaniment. In order to achieve balance between the organ and the ensemble of winds and strings, the use of plenum-style registration on the organs at St. Nicholas and at St. Thomas was necessary.

The variants in the different versions of the extended keyboard solo passage in the first movement of the D-minor concerto, BWV 1052/1052a (mm. 165ff.), illustrate various stages in its evolution. Example 4 presents the transition to the Arpeggio in abbreviated notation. The notation of a distinct bass line in B and its spatial separation from the manual part may suggest the use of the organ pedal. Example 5 provides a synopsis of the Arpeggio in versions A–C, with the revised harpsichord solo part written out and placed an octave lower. Example 6 shows the string score of the same passage. In version A, the strings do not accompany the solo part. The string accompaniment in version B is scored for two violins and viola only, with the continuo part *tacet*. In version C, Bach writes out a full four-part string accompaniment and adds a pedal point over five measures to the chromatic harmonies in the upper voices.

These variants illustrate the effectiveness of various keyboard instruments for different purposes. The Leipzig cantatas with obbligato organ were performed in large churches with two thousand or more worshippers present, while the venues and audiences for the harpsichord concertos were significantly smaller. For keyboard concertos with orchestral accompaniment, the organ has clear advantages for public presentations

Ex. 4. Concerto in D Minor, BWV 1052/1, mm. 165–69

Ex. 5. Concerto in D Minor, BWV 1052/1, mm. 166–67

Ex. 6. Concerto in D Minor, BWV 1052/1, mm. 166–69, string parts in versions A (tacet), B, and C

in large spaces, whereas the harpsichord is better suited for more intimate settings. In this light, Bach's choice of the organ loft of St. Sophia Church as a venue for his public concerts with the Dresden court capelle was both logical and practical.

Although the content of the 1725 Dresden recitals mentioned above remains entirely unknown, the inclusion of early concerto versions of BWV 1052 and 1053 for solo organ is plausible because of the chronological proximity of the related cantatas. Of the two works, the D-minor concerto, although clearly representing an older piece most likely from the post-1714 Weimar years, had not lost its special appeal as a daring and flashy showpiece requiring unparalleled virtuosity. Even later, around 1738, it was still deemed so exemplary and attractive by Bach that he chose it to head the collection of concertos in P 234. In contrast, BWV 1053, a more recent composition, would have represented a modern counterpart to the earlier work, its *Siciliano* exemplifying an advanced harmonic language of novel expressivity.[21]

In addition, the earlier version of BWV 1053 for organ solo would have been the perfect match for the Silbermann organ at St. Sophia's, an instrument different from those available to Bach in Leipzig. The keys of the movements of this concerto correspond nicely with the report about Bach's playing "in all keys," for the keys of E major

21. For more on this and the topic of the subsequent paragraph, see Wolff, "Sicilianos and Organ Recitals," 104–14.

and C-sharp minor (with four sharps each) were at the extreme end of the spectrum normally present in compositions of the time. In fact, an E-major concerto for organ solo would help solve the many problems that have long plagued scholars, including the question of the original key of this concerto:

1. The key of E major (not E-flat or D major) would explain the frequent copying errors (entry of notes originally a second too high) in the ripieno parts (notated in D major) of the autograph score of BWV 169.
2. The temperament of the organ of St. Sophia's would have facilitated playing in all keys. The instrument (tuned in "Dresden" *Cammerton*) featured the unusual manual compass C, D-d´´ and thus accommodated the highest note in BWV 1053/1: c♯´´. (Bach's Leipzig organs tuned in choir pitch had the normal manual compass, C, D-c´´.)
3. In cantata BWV 169 Bach had to transpose the first two movements a whole tone down from E major and C-sharp minor, respectively, for two reasons: first, to accommodate the *Chorton* tuning of the organ a whole step above the *Cammerton* of the other instruments; and second, to make available the tone c♯´´ (b´ *Chorton*) on the Leipzig organs which extended up only to c´.´ To make this possible, he transposed the autograph score of the cantata movement down a whole tone to D (*Cammerton*), with the obbligato organ part in C major (*Chorton*), thus lowering the highest note to b´´.
4. The third movement of the concerto required no downward transposition, as the highest note in the solo part of the Sinfonia BWV 49 is b´´.
5. The melodic figuration and passagework in the E major and C-sharp minor concerto movements are entirely consistent with idiomatic keyboard writing. Neither key presents difficulties, and the uninterrupted chains of sixteenth notes that would present breathing problems for any wind instrument can easily be accommodated. The left-hand part needed no elaboration, since it would have been improvised by the composer. The extensive revisions made to the solo part subsequently in P 234 may well reflect Bach's improvisatorial practice in treating the left-hand part and not necessarily a new approach conceptually.

The chronological problems are also solved if this proposed original E-major organ concerto is seen in the context of the *siciliano* arias of the second and third Leipzig cantata cycles, which appear for the first time in the fall of 1724. Analytical observations that BWV 1053 adopted certain formal and stylistic features from the innovative *Concerti a cinque*, opus 9 by Tommaso Albinoni (Amsterdam, 1722), as suggested by Gregory Butler, also support a likely date of composition for this concerto in the mid-1720s.[22]

22. For a dating to 1725, see Gregory Butler, "Bach the Cobbler: The Origins of J. S. Bach's E-Major Concerto (BWV 1053)," in *Bach Perspectives 7: J. S. Bach's Concerted Ensemble Music: The Concerto*, edited by Gregory Butler (Urbana: University of Illinois Press, 2008), 1–20.

As we possess no musical sources for the two hypothetical "Dresden" organ concertos, there remains the question of the actual musical text of both the solo and orchestral parts. The four cantata scores incorporating the six concerto movements indicate that the instrumental settings were integrated without substantive compositional changes. The orchestral scoring was augmented for performance in Leipzig by the addition of woodwinds to the original strings-only accompaniment: two regular hautbois plus taille in BWV 146/1 and 188/1 (compare with BWV 1052/1 and 3); two hautbois d'amour and taille in BWV 169/1 and one hautbois d'amour in BWV 49/1 (compare with BWV 1053/1, 3). The keyboard solo parts required few if any adjustments.

To sum up: the two first entries in the autograph manuscript P 234 (ca. 1738), the D-minor and E-major harpsichord concertos (BWV 1052–1053) and their related movements in cantatas 49, 146, 169, and 188 (1726–1727) provide considerable evidence for their origin as keyboard concertos in the same two keys—not as concertos for violin, oboe, or any other solo instrument, as has long been supposed. Idiomatic keyboard style and figuration throughout, as well as the compass of the solo parts, provide strong arguments in favor of the keyboard and organ in particular for the purpose of a public recital. Moreover, the cantata sinfonias for organ from the later 1720s and harpsichord concerto versions of the 1730s suggest the concept of a dual function, that is, the concertos were designed for performance on either harpsichord or organ. The choice of instrument would be determined by the performance venue: a church recital or a more intimate chamber music setting. Bach the performer-composer, who was equally comfortable on either instrument, wrote such works primarily for his own use, sketching out a solo part and making appropriate adjustments and improvisatory elaborations as needed at either harpsichord or organ. The revised harpsichord solo parts in P 234, which in all likelihood were written for use by others and possibly for publication, have no equivalent in the surviving cantata materials. As Bach himself had no need for fully elaborated organ parts, organists today are left to their own ingenuity. Yet the harpsichord versions may well serve as a general guide for the proper use of the left hand; the continuo line of the cantata scores, meanwhile, suggests an intermittent, pointed, and musically sensible use of the pedal, notably for the ritornello sections.

The Choir Loft as Chamber

Concerted Movements by Bach from the Mid- to Late 1720s

Gregory Butler

Bach's activities as composer and performer for the Collegium Musicum in Leipzig have always been seen as distinct from those for the principal churches in Leipzig. But at the same time that Bach was engaged in parodying secular vocal compositions, transforming them into church cantatas, he was also adapting for church performances preexisting instrumental concerted movements with obbligato organ now substituting as solo melody instrument in various sinfonias, arias, and choruses. The aim of this study is to demonstrate that after late May 1725—when the steady flow of new cantata compositions by Bach ceased and the secular arena of the *ordinaire* and *extraordinaire* performances of the Collegium, especially during the Leipzig fairs, became just as important for Bach as the weekly performances of concerted vocal music at the *Haupgottesdienst* in Leipzig's two principal churches—the two spheres of activity were, at times, closely interrelated.

As a paradigm for this interrelationship, I have chosen to focus on the Concerto in E Major for harpsichord and strings, BWV 1053, which comes down to us in the autograph score SBB-PK *Mus. ms. Bach P 234*, assembled ca. 1738. Its three movements appear more than a decade earlier in two cantatas from Bach's third *Jahrgang* featuring obbligato organ: the first two as movements 1 and 5 of the cantata *Gott soll allein mein Herze haben*, BWV 169 (October 20, 1726), and the third as movement 1 of the cantata *Ich geh und suche mit Verlangen*, BWV 49 (November 3, 1726). All three movements have antecedents in earlier concerted instrumental movements,[1] for they have clearly been copied from *Vorlagen* into the autograph scores of the two cantatas in question: SBB-PK *Mus. ms. Bach P 93* and SBB-PK *Mus. ms. Bach P 111*, respectively. Werner Breig, editor

1. See Ulrich Siegele, *Kompositionsweise und Bearbeitungstechnik in der Instrumentalmusik Johann Sebastian Bachs*, Tübinger Beiträge zur Musikwissenschaft 3, edited by Georg von Dadelsen (Neuhausen-Stuttgart: Hänssler-Verlag, 1975), 137, and Werner Breig, NBA VII/4, KB, 87.

of BWV 1053 for the *Neue Bach-Ausgabe*, is understandably hesitant when it comes to any hard-and-fast conclusions concerning the source history of the work,[2] which as we shall see is highly problematic.

Thorniest in this regard is the opening movement. In the ripieno parts of BWV 169/1 in P 93, a plethora of transposition corrections of notes originally entered a tone too high and then corrected down by a step leaves no doubt that these D-major parts were transcribed from a *Vorlage* in E major.[3] The organo obbligato treble and bass/continuo parts are another matter entirely. They are pristine in appearance, which is somewhat surprising, since one would expect, at the very least, signs of transposition of the treble part down a third into C major. (The Leipzig organs were pitched at *Chorton*, a step higher than *Cammerton*.) One possible explanation for this anomaly is that Bach adopted the expedient of reading the part of the solo melody instrument in the *Vorlage* in soprano clef while transcribing it into C major in P 93, but this does not account for the clean appearance of the bass/continuo part. Or, is it possible that the *Vorlage* for these two parts was in C major and so no transposition was required? Then again, there are two transposition errors, one in each of the treble and bass/continuo parts, of notes originally entered a step too high but corrected down by step,[4] suggesting that these lines were copied from a *Vorlage* not in E major but in D major. If so, does this constitute evidence that the original *Vorlage* was scored for solo organ (written in D major but sounding in E major), or that these parts were transcribed from a D-major source in which both the solo melody instrument and continuo were at *Cammerton* pitch?

A detail in the ripieno parts of the E major version of the movement (in P 234) may offer a clue. In the second violin part there are a handful of transposition corrections of notes originally entered a step too low,[5] a concentration of such corrections that appears in no other part. Does this indicate that the *Vorlage* for this part was not in E major but rather in D major, and if so, what was the nature of this *Vorlage*? Was it a part? Why was this source necessary?

The source history of movement 3 would seem to be the least contentious of all. It is clear that an E-major *Vorlage* composed between 1722 and 1726 was the basis for the readings of the movement in BWV 49/1 and in BWV1053/3.[6] But in the set of parts

2. See NBA VII/4, KB, 132–37.

3. See Matthias Wendt's commentary in NBA I/24, KB, 60–61.

4. *Ibid.*, 60.

5. See Breig, NBA VII/4, KB, 66–71.

6. For my argument for a dating of the original version of this movement to this period, see Gregory Butler, "J. S. Bach's Reception of the Mature Concertos of Tomaso Albinoni," in *Bach Studies* 2, edited by Daniel R. Melamed (Cambridge: Cambridge University Press, 1995), 20–46.

for BWV 49, SBB-PK *Mus. ms. Bach St 55*, the viola part for the opening movement is in D major. Ulrich Bartels, in his edition of the cantata for the *Neue Bach-Ausgabe*, remarks simply that the part is in D major, adding somewhat cryptically that it "was probably copied from the *Vorlage* for the concerto."[7] If this is the case, then why was the part transposed into D major, and what is it doing in a set of parts in E major?

I believe that the answer to this question may lie in a previously unexplained detail in the part. A bass clef without key signature has been entered at the beginning of the first system, where it is crowded by the correct alto clef with signature of two sharps entered subsequently (see plate 1). I would suggest that this is not a matter of the scribe having entered the wrong clef and catching himself before entering the incorrect key signature but rather that we are dealing here with a transposing part.[8] If one reads the part as written in the bass clef, then the tonic pitch, D, becomes E, a seventh below. In other words, the bass clef functions as a cue to the violist to transpose the part into E major. Several notes originally entered a tone too high and subsequently corrected down a step are to be expected in parts transposed down from a *Vorlage* in E major. Yet I would argue that the very existence of the St 55 viola part points to at least one performance of the movement in D major sometime before the first performance of BWV 49 in November 1726.

To expand a bit on this scenario: since he already had a part for this movement in D major from a previous performance, Bach simply reused the D-major part instead of having the part recopied and transposed into E major for the cantata performance. Because it was copied on a single face of a leaf of paper with the other face blank, Bach had the copyist enter the cue for the performer at the beginning of the first system and the indicator "Aria tac[et]" at the end of the final system. The copyist then turned the leaf to begin copying the movements of the cantata following the sinfonia, beginning on the verso face with movement 3, the next movement that includes viola in its scoring. In other words, the single leaf prepared for an earlier performance of the movement in D major became the first leaf of the viola part (from St 55) used for the performance of BWV 49 on November 3, 1726. Watermark evidence suggests that the earlier D-major performance took place sometime between the last week in June and

7. "... wurde möglicherweise aus der Konzertvorlage kopiert." Ulrich Bartels, NBA I/25, KB, 100.

8. Since Bach's adaptation of previously composed concerted instrumental movements as sinfonias for his Leipzig church cantatas rarely involved transposition, the need for such transposing parts did not arise. (An exception is the sinfonia that opens the cantata *Ich steh mit einem Fuß im Grabe*, BWV 156, first performed on January 23, 1729, originally in F major but transposed to A-flat major as the second movement of BWV 1056, whose performing materials include no transposing parts.) Thus, it would not be surprising if this were a unique instance of the procedure.

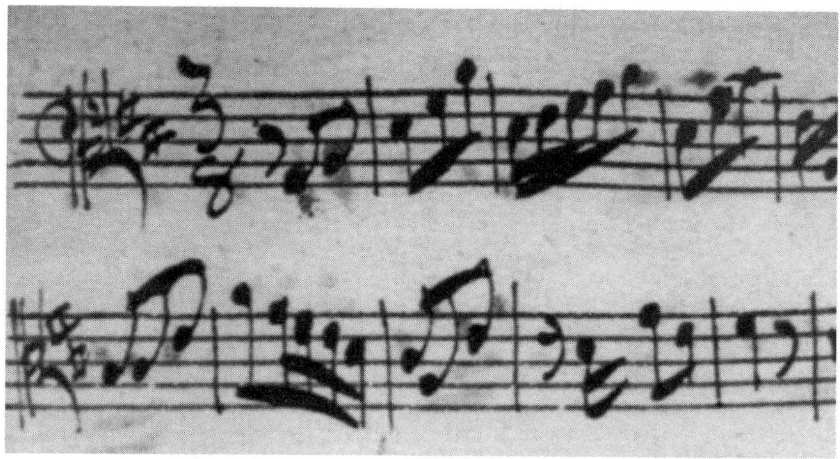

Plate 1. Detail from viola part of BWV 49/1 (SBB-PK: *Mus. ms. Bach St 55*. Reproduced with permission.)

early November of the same year.[9] If indeed that earlier performance of the entire three-movement concerto relied on D-major parts, the source from which Bach transcribed the second violin part of the first movement in P 234 may have been altered in the same manner: in the case of a part in D major notated in treble clef, reading the music as written in the alto clef would result in the transposition of the music from D into E major.

Thus far, Bach scholars without exception have posited the existence of a concerto for melody instrument, strings, and continuo in E/E-flat major as the *Vorlage* for BWV 1053. But this argument is no longer tenable. Although the *Vorlagen* for the opening and closing movements (sources [**X**] and [**Y**]) were both in E major, a period of almost a decade separates their composition, and since the *Vorlage* for the middle movement (source [**Z**]) was, from its inception, in B minor, one can only conclude that the three sources are independent entities.[10] But if, as I have argued above, there were transposing ripieno parts for the outer movements of this concerto, then they, along with the middle movement that needed no transposition, could also have been performed as

9. The paper with the watermark "ICF" (Weiss 132) on which the movement was copied was used by Bach between June 23, 1726, and January 5, 1727. See Alfred Dürr, *Zur Chronologie Bachs Leipziger Vokalwerke* (Kassel: Bärenreiter, 1976), 138–39.

10. See my own "Bach the Cobbler: The Origins of J. S. Bach's E-Major Concerto (BWV 1053)" in *Bach Perspectives 7: J. S. Bach's Concerted Ensemble Music: The Concerto*, edited by Gregory Butler (Urbana: University of Illinois Press, 2008), 1–20.

Figure 1. Stemma of the Source History of the Concerto for Cembalo, Strings, and Continuo in E Major, BWV 1053

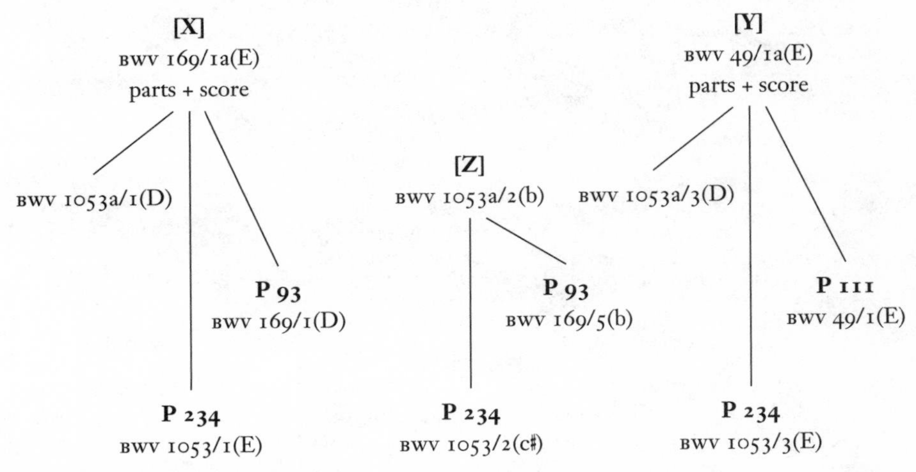

a D-major concerto with oboe d'amore as the most likely solo melody instrument.[11] In such a scenario, it is likely that the middle movement of this concerto was, in fact, the B-minor *Vorlage* for BWV 169/5 and BWV 1053/2 (see figure 1).[12]

Christoph Wolff has advanced the hypothesis that an early version of BWV 1053—for solo organ, strings, and continuo in E major—was one of the concertos Bach performed when he gave two concerts on the new Silbermann organ in the Sophienkirche, Dresden, on September 19 and 20, 1725.[13] Though in general his argument is compelling, I would suggest that this concerto, if it ever existed, would have to have been in D major, not in E major. The existence of transposing parts makes plausible an earlier concerto in

11. Bruce Haynes has concluded that this concerto produces a satisfactory result only when played in D major, producing a solo part from A-b', the effective range of the oboe d'amore. Bruce Haynes, "Johann Sebastian Bachs Oboenkonzerte," *Bach-Jahrbuch* 78 (1992): 42. Noting instances in movement 3 (mm. 222–23) where, in the key of D major, Violin 1 and 2 would dip down to F♯, Haynes suggests that the entire passage from mm. 222–25 was originally an octave higher in these parts. The precipitous two-octave descent in all three ripieno string parts at the beginning of m. 222 lends credence to his supposition.

12. Christoph Wolff has argued convincingly on stylistic grounds that the middle movement, a siciliano, dates to the period after the fall of 1724. See Christoph Wolff, "Sicilianos and Organ Recitals: Observations on J. S. Bach's Concertos," in *Bach Perspectives* 7, 101–4.

13. Wolff, "Sicilianos and Organ Recitals," 97–114.

D major; moreover, there is no source evidence pointing to the existence of a version of movement 2 in C-sharp minor before its transposition as BWV 1053/2 in P 234.

Just as important, counter to Wolff's assertion that "the earlier version of BWV 1053 for organ solo [in E major] would have been the perfect match for the Silbermann organ at St. Sophia's,"[14] is the unfavorable reception of Silbermann's tuning by organists and organ builders. Notable among these is Georg Andreas Sorge, who, referring to "many organ and instrument builders, even including Mr. Gottfried Silbermann," remarks of their tuning systems that "of the twenty-four keys one hardly finds four that are not sullied by nasty and unbearably sharp thirds, not to speak of the completely unusable fifth g♯—d♯." Later in the same treatise Sorge states that "the fifth, g♯—d♯, sounds unbearable" and even invokes Bach on the subject: "Silbermann's way of tempering cannot be maintained in today's practice. . . . In his four bad triads a raw, wild or (as Capellmeister Bach in Leipzig calls it) barbaric nature is contained."[15] The "unusable fifth" singled out by Sorge, and certainly one of his "four bad triads," the G-sharp triad, is prominent in both the keys of E major and C-sharp minor. I find it more likely that if Bach did play an earlier version of the concerto in Dresden, it would have been a D-major performance from transposing string parts, such as the viola part of BWV 49/3 in St 55.

Since the Silbermann organ in the Sophienkirche was a *Cammerton* instrument, the solo part would have been in the same key as the ripieno parts. In D major the highest note reached in the organo obbligato treble part in movement one, the c♯'' in measure 112, would seem to argue against the possibility of a D-major version; but it should be kept in mind that this note is a result of the transposition to the upper octave of the first sixteenths of the three groups of four sixteenths, which opens the measure in the later revised reading of this passage (example 1b). In the earlier version preserved in BWV 1053/1 (example 1a), where the notes in question appear at the lower octave, the entire passage is playable on an organ at *Chorton* pitch;[16] even the later version would

14. *Ibid.*, 111.

15. " . . . viele von denen Herren Orgel-und Instrumentmachern, auch den berühmten Herrn Gottfried Silbermann nicht ausgenommen, . . . man von denen 24. Tonarten kaum 4. findet, die nicht mit bösen und unleidlich scharffen Terzen, der ganz unbrauchbaren Quint gis:dis, nicht einmahl zu gedencken, beschmitzet sind."

" . . . daß die Quinte gs:ds unleidlich über sich schwebet, welches keinesweges zu leugnen; . . . Die Silbermannische Art zu temperiren, kan bey heutiger Praxi nicht bestehen. . . . In denen 4. schlimmen *Triadibus* . . . ist ein rauhes wildes, oder, wie Herr Capellmeister Bach in Leipzig redet, ein barbarisches Wesen enthalten." Georg Andreas Sorge, *Gespräch . . . von der Prätorianischen, Prinzischen, Werckmeisterischen, Neidhardtischen und Silbermannischen Temperatur* (Lobenstein, 1748), 10, 21.

16. At the same time it is interesting that the version of the following cadence (at the end of m. 112 in BWV 169/1) is less complicated rhythmically than that in BWV 1053/1. But this is typical of the version for harpsichord, where such superficial revisions are the rule rather than the exception.

Ex. 1a. Concerto in E Major BWV 1053/1 (transposed), mm. 112–13

Ex. 1b. Cantata 169/1, organ treble part, mm. 112–13

have been playable on the Silbermann organ at the Sophienkirche, whose compass extended up to d′′′.

I would suggest that it was in the course of transposing the organo obbligato treble part into C major (for a *Chorton* organ in Leipzig) that Bach revised the original reading given in example 1a to arrive at the later reading. The original reading of this measure in source [**X**], the E-major *Vorlage*, was the reading later entered into BWV 1053/1 in P 234.

I would like to put forward the possibility that an early D-major version of this concerto, BWV 1053a, for solo oboe d'amore or organ, plus the cantata versions of its three movements (with obbligato organ) as BWV 169/1, BWV 169/5 and BWV 49/1 all came into existence around the same time and that they form a matrix of pieces performed in the fall of 1726. Given the dating of the transposing viola part from St 55, performances of the D-major concerto as a whole or of its movements singly as sinfonias,[17] in versions for solo oboe d'amore and/or solo keyboard (either organ or harpsichord), may well have been on the program at one or more of the bi-weekly performances of the Collegium during the Michaelmas Fair in October 1726.[18]

17. We know that the sinfonia as a genre was an important component of Collegium performances. See Andreas Glöckner, "Bachs Leipziger *Collegium musicum* und seine Vorgeschichte" in *Die Welt der Bach-Kantaten 2: Johann Sebastian Bachs weltliche Kantaten*, edited by Christoph Wolff and Ton Koopman (Stuttgart and Kassel: Metzler/Bärenreiter, 1997), 109.

18. It is clear that Bach was a participant in Collegium performances both as performer and composer at least as early as 1724, the year after his arrival in Leipzig. Heinrich Nikolaus Gerber, a student of Bach's, reports having heard "much excellent church music and many a concert under Bach's direction" ("manche vortrefliche Kirchenmusik und manches Conzert unter Bachs Direktion") as early as the second half of 1724. Ernst Ludwig Gerber, *Historisch-Biographishes Lexicon der Tonkünstler*, I (Leipzig, 1790), col. 490. Further, Bach had his copyists prepare a set of parts for the Ouverture in C Major, BWV 1066 (SBB-PK *Mus. ms. Bach St 152*), ostensibly for a performance of the Collegium, in the same year.

Another group of works from the late 1720s comprising sinfonias for obbligato organ and a related harpsichord concerto suggests a similar interpretation. A movement performed in the spring of 1729 has some parallels with BWV 169/1: the sinfonia that opens part 2 of the wedding cantata *Herr Gott, Beherrscher aller Dinge*, BWV 120a. This sinfonia, a D-major arrangement for obbligato organ and ripieno strings of the Preludio from the Third Partita for Solo Violin in E Major, BWV 1006, involves the same transposition as that observed in BWV 169/1. Even though only the conclusion of the movement has survived as a fragment in the autograph score of the cantata (SBB-PK *Mus. ms. P 670*), it is clear that the string and organ bass parts constitute a composing score while that of the solo organ treble part is a fair copy. Bach first entered the obbligato organ treble part on the next-to-bottom staff of the score and then composed the ripieno string and organ bass parts, filling in the upper three staves and bottom staff as he went along. The process for transposing the obbligato treble part was in all likelihood the same as that suggested above for the transcription of the treble part in the autograph fair copy of BWV 169/1: Bach read the sonata part in the soprano clef while transcribing it into treble clef as the right-hand of the obbligato organ part, thus transposing it from E major into C major for a *Chorton* organ.

How does the Sinfonia BWV 120a fit into the performance schedule of Bach's chamber works in the late 1720s? Sometime toward the end of 1727, Georg Heinrich Ludwig Schwanberg, *Cammermusicus* at the court of Braunschweig-Wolffenbüttel, arrived in Leipzig to study with Bach.[19] Schwanberg was close to Bach and to the Bach family as a whole, having acted before his arrival in Leipzig as Bach's agent in Braunschweig for the sale of Partitas 2 and 3, BWV 826-827; he also stood as godfather to the Bachs' daughter Regina Johanna in October 1728.[20] An accomplished violinist, Schwanberg can be expected to have served as concertist in Bach's cantata performances, and he was surely also a regular attendee of Schott's Collegium Musicum during his time in Leipzig. During this same period (1727–31), Anna Magdalena Bach prepared copies of both the sonatas and partitas for unaccompanied violin, BWV 1001–1006, and the sonatas for solo violoncello, BWV 1007–1012.[21] Schwanberg penned the title pages of these copies, suggesting that he may have commissioned them. The likely window for

19. For a detailed biography of Schwanberg, an account of his close ties with Bach and the Bach family, and his relationship with Anna Magdalena Bach's copies of the sonatas and partitas for solo violin and the sonatas for solo violoncello, see Hans Joachim Schulze, *Studien zur Bach-Überlieferung im 18. Jahrhundert* (Leipzig: Peters, 1984), 95–101.

20. BDOK II, 169 and 183.

21. Bach used paper with the watermark "MA mittlere Form" (Weiß 122) between October 17, 1727, and December 2, 1731.

the arrangement (BWV 120a/1) of the Preludio (BWV 1006/1)—between late April and late May 1729—suggests that Bach was revisiting his solo violin works at this time. There also seems to be a close chronological link between this arrangement and the copies prepared for Schwanberg by Anna Magdalena Bach. If Schwanberg's copies were prepared at around the same time, then surely he was studying and playing the works not only privately but perhaps publicly at performances of the Collegium Musicum.

In this regard, *Wir müssen durch viel Trübsal*, BWV 146, and *Ich habe meine Zuversicht*, BWV 188—which, like the Sinfonia BWV 120a/4, feature obbligato organ—are also of particular interest. Movements one and two of the former, the opening sinfonia and the chorus "Wir müssen durch viel Trübsal," form a clear parallel with BWV 169/1 and 169/5 in that they constitute a fast-slow movement pair, which shows up later in P 234 as the first and second movements of the Concerto in D Minor for harpsichord and strings, BWV 1052; the sinfonia that opens BWV 188, paralleling the opening movement of BWV 49, appears as the closing movement of BWV 1052. All three movements may ultimately stem from concerted movements for solo violin and strings; scholars have long supposed that they once formed a homogeneous three-movement cycle as a D-minor violin concerto.[22]

Unfortunately, the original performing materials for neither cantata have survived, and the score for BWV 146 comes down to us only in a late copy, making the date of its first performance difficult to pin down with any precision.[23] The only available autograph source material is a fragment of BWV 188/1 consisting of the final thirty-eight measures. Thus a comprehensive, detailed study of the source history of BWV 1052 is not possible, and we have no evidence that a D-minor concerto for solo violin ever existed. The *Vorlagen* for the outer movements may have their origins in sinfonias or opening movements to serenatas performed in Cöthen; the middle movement, with its arguably archaic ostinato bass treatment, may go back to a sinfonia from the late Weimar years.

The existence of a D-minor concerto for solo violin, even if it could be substantiated, surely does not constitute grounds for the dating of the first performances of BWV 146 and BWV 188 in the same year. But the presence in Leipzig of a player of Schwanberg's caliber during 1728 and his performance of Bach's works for solo violin in a chamber setting during the same period may have influenced Bach's decision to arrange the *Vorlagen* of all three movements for obbligato organ in BWV 146 and BWV 188. The

22. For a summary, see Breig, NBA VII/4, KB, 52. But for an alternative view, see Wolff, "Organ Recitals and Sicilianos," 109–11, and his essay in this volume, "Did J. S. Bach Write Organ Concertos?"

23. Alfred Dürr has given Jubilate Sunday 1726–28 as possible dates for the first performance: see Dürr, *Zur Chronologie*, 87, 166. Since the libretto by Picander did not appear in print until 1728, preference has been given to April 18, 1728: see BC II, 653.

solo violin part of the concerto's first movement, which served as the *Vorlage* for BWV 146/1 and BWV 1052/1, is without doubt more technically demanding than any of the allegro movements in the three extant concerti for solo violin(s), BWV 1041–1043, and arguably the most highly virtuosic music for the instrument in the composer's oeuvre—with the exception of certain movements from the solo sonatas and partitas such as BWV 1006/1. Did its initial success as a virtuoso vehicle for Schwanberg prompt Bach to adapt this concerto for keyboard?

At the very least, we might suppose that Schwanberg performed versions of all three movements—whether as reprises of earlier sinfonias or as movements of a newly assembled D-minor concerto for solo violin—at one of the bi-weekly performances given by the Collegium during the Easter Fair period of 1728 and/or during the following Michaelmas Fair period, respectively. Bach's arrangement of BWV 1006/1 might be a clue that Schwanberg was still in Leipzig the following spring. In 1729 the Easter Fair stretched beyond the middle of May, so a performance of BWV 1006 at a Collegium concert during the last two weeks of April or the first two weeks of May is a distinct possibility. To extend this line of reasoning: in the same way that the concerted movements for obbligato organ from the post-Trinity period in 1726 form a clutch of arrangements of concerted instrumental movements, so Schwanberg's stay in Leipzig from October 1727 through (?)May 1729 may have given rise to a group of arrangements for obbligato organ of concerted instrumental movements originally for solo violin.

Most of the cantatas with organ obbligato are solo or dialog cantatas and, except for concluding *cantional* chorale settings, have no large-scale choral movements. Both stylistically and conceptually, these works represent a startling departure from the cantatas of Bach's first two yearly cycles in Leipzig. Instead of directing the *chorus musicus* from the front, Bach the organist was one of a small but select group of *Cammermusici*,[24] just as he was when seated at the harpsichord as composer and performer of his serenatas in Cöthen and with the Collegium in Leipzig. As performer of the obbligato organ part, Bach was assuming (like Schwanberg) the role of virtuoso *Cammermusicus*, a role radically different from that of *Thomascantor*. In so doing, the choir loft became the chamber. This shift has to do not only with musical style and substance but also with sonority, since with these pieces the organ came to prominence as an

24. It is striking that not a single *organo* part survives from any of the first performances of the cantatas with obbligato organ from the Leipzig period. Bach scholars have concluded from this that Bach himself performed these parts, playing them on the large organs in the St. Thomas and St. Nicholas Churches from the autograph score. See Laurence Dreyfus, *Bach's Continuo Group: Players and Practices in His Vocal Works* (Cambridge, Mass.: Harvard University Press, 1987), 64. In taking the organist's place for performances of these works, Bach's back would have been toward the singers and instrumentalists; the prefect would presumably have conducted performances of these cantatas.

obbligato instrument in an intimate chamber configuration. At the same time, the organ took on a new and special relationship with the other musicians. Now on an equal footing with the other melody instruments, it transcended its normal role as part of the continuo group.

The picture of Bach painted here comes into sharper focus when one considers his performances before dignitaries of the Electoral Saxon court on the Silbermann organ in the Dresden Sophienkirche on September 19 and 20, 1725, referred to earlier in this essay. More than a year before his first performances in Leipzig of cantatas with obbligato organ, Bach had initiated a "choir loft as chamber" approach to organ performance—and apparently to great acclaim. Feelings of confinement as Leipzig's Cantor may have been brought on by or exacerbated by the Dresden trip; Bach's 1726 publication of the first of six keyboard partitas (republished as *Clavierübung I* in 1731) may likewise represent an effort to broaden his horizons. His appearance during the Leipzig fairs as director and/or soloist—performing different versions of the same concerted instrumental movements for the chamber and for the church—may have been part of the same effort: to reach a wider audience than that to which he had devoted himself during his first two years in Leipzig.

Music from Heaven

An Eighteenth-Century Context for Cantatas with Obbligato Organ

Matthew Cron*

Of the almost two hundred surviving church cantatas by Johann Sebastian Bach, eighteen contain movements where the organist steps out of his normal role of continuo player and becomes a concertist. Modern scholarship has considered such compositions primarily from two perspectives: a historiographical perspective places them in the larger context of the history of the keyboard concerto, while a compositional perspective considers them as examples of the arrangement and reworking of previous musical material. The following study examines these works from the perspective of an original listener (in other words, a member of the congregation) to describe how a particular yet widespread way of thinking about the organ created a fruitful context for this new type of cantata in the early eighteenth century.

No member of Bach's Leipzig congregation would have had the historical hindsight to link concerted organ movements in church to the emerging keyboard concerto. Even those who might have heard Bach's harpsichord concertos at Zimmermann's coffeehouse in the 1730s may not have remembered hearing organ versions of a half-dozen movements in a group of cantatas from 1726. While some Leipzigers may have recognized concerto form in these six movements, Bach's extant cantatas contain twenty-seven other movements, mostly arias, that use the organ in a non-concerted manner. In these, the organ functions in the same manner as a solo flute, oboe, or violin in arias from other cantatas—that is, as an instrumental obbligato. Nor would eighteenth-century listeners have had the wide range of assocations for the organ as we do—from the concert hall to the ball park. Because Bach's contemporaries encountered the organ primarily within a church context, their understanding of the instrument would have relied on its striking visual impact, its use in worship (especially in hymn

* The author would like to acknowledge the invaluable advice of Matthew Dirst in preparing this essay for publication.

singing), and on what was said about it in devotionals, sermons, writings on music, and in cantata texts, especially those in which the organ is featured prominently. The one constant in all these various media was a strong association of the organ with Heaven: this instrument, above all others, prepares one for service in the heavenly choir while providing a source of solace and joy on earth.

During the Baroque Age the decoration of organs with the symbols of Heaven—angels, clouds, sun, and stars—provided a powerful visual context for the instrument.[1] The most frequent symbol of Heaven found on these instruments is the angel, which can be depicted in a variety of ways, from carved busts to full-body statues or child-like *putti*.[2] Angels of judgement (typically with trumpets) are also common, as are angel musicians of all sorts playing violins, trombones, harps, even timpani.[3] Angels and clouds were also frequently painted on organ doors or on walls behind organs, reminding the faithful that even when not in use, these instruments were somehow part of Heaven on earth. One particularly fine example of this kind of decoration can be found in an organ that was familiar to both Bach and Georg Philipp Telemann. An engraving of the Donat organ of the New Church in Leipzig, as rebuilt by Johann Scheibe in 1722, depicts two small angels on the sides of the top of the organ case and two large angels in flight amid clouds painted on the vaulted wall behind the organ (see plate 1[OBH, 57]).[4] Seen from the main floor of the church, the organ appeared as if in Heaven accompanied by angels. Explicit or implicit connections between the Psalms and Baroque organ decoration were common, as can be seen in a well-known engraving of the 1714 Silbermann organ in Freiberg Cathedral.[5] This engraving depicts a performance of concerted music with the new organ, whose case includes two small angels at the very top and two trumpeting angels surrounding the Oberwerk. On the sides of the Brustwerk are an angel playing an organ and another playing drums, both seated on heavenly clouds.[6]

1. Such decorations can be found on organs throughout Europe as well as on those organs associated with Bach. Examples of the latter can be found in OBH.

2. For example, the Compenius organ at the Prediger Church in Erfurt (OBH, 106), the Hantelmann organ in the Cathedral of Lübeck (OBH, 120), and the Müller organ in St. Mary Church in Cöthen (OBH, 44) respectively.

3. For example, the Niehoff/Johannsen/Stellwagen organ of St. Catherine Church in Hamburg (OBH, 35) and the Hildebrandt organ at St. Jacobi Church in Sangerhausen (OBH, 39).

4. This instrument was originally built in 1703–4 and its first organist was Georg Philipp Telemann.

5. See OBH, 109.

6. Several verses of Psalm 150, which praises God "with pipe and drum," are quoted on a banner on the top of the engraving. St. Cecilia appears in many an organ decoration as a player. Examples of painted doors where one door depicts St. Cecilia and the opposite door depicts King David playing a harp can be found on organs in Germany, France, Switzerland, Italy, the

Plate 1. Engraving of the Donat organ of the New Church in Leipzig, rebuilt by Johann Scheibe in 1722

Other celestial symbols found on organs of this time include the sun and stars. The former is most prominently represented on the Casparini organ (the so-called "Sun Organ") in the Church of Sts. Peter and Paul in Görlitz as well as the Wagner organs in St. Mary Church, Berlin, and the Garrison Church in Potsdam, which also had animated angels that were activated by drawknobs for fanfaring and drumming angels, respectively.[7] The Casparini organ had revolving suns, angels, and birds, all of which

Netherlands, Austria, Slovakia, and Slovenia. See Anneke Hut et al., *Die bemalten Orgelflügel in Europa* (Rotterdam: Stichting Organa Historica, 2001): 39, 86, 107, 113, 186, 191, and variously.

7. See OBH, 28, 103, and 81–82, respectively. A moveable sun is also found on the Contius organ in the Market Church in Halle. At the time that Bach, Johann Kuhnau, and Christian Freiderich Rolle examined this newly built instrument in 1716, the "moveable sun [was] operable from a stop in the Oberwerk" but several other accessory stops had not been completed. See OBH, 144.

played specific pitches.[8] Such an aural reminder of the celestial object is also found in the Cymbelstern stops present on most of the organs associated with Bach, including the Stertzing organ in St. George Church in Eisenach, which had two Cymbelstern whose stars and bells could be operated separately,[9] and also on organs in every city where Bach held a post. The constant sound of bells was a reminder of Psalm 150's exhortation to praise God with the sound of cymbals, a sentiment echoed in the final verse of the familiar Christmas hymn *In dulci jubilo*: "Where is joy, nowhere more than there? There the angels sing new songs, and there the bells ring in the King's court; O that we were there!"[10] The *Vogelgesang*, a common "toy stop" on German instruments of this time, conjured similar associations for generations of listeners.[11] While one might regard a stop that imitates warbling birds as a mere novelty, its spiritual significance is discussed in organ dedication sermons, one of which claims that the sound of the Vogelgesang causes one to "take wing, rising from the earthly lot, and intone the heavenly music: *Gloria in Excelsis Deo!* Glory be to God in the highest!"[12] Additional observations from dedication sermons will concern us presently.

The physical location of the organ also reinforced its status as a heavenly instrument: even in relatively small churches with modest organs, placement was usually as high as

8. In his description of this newly built instrument, the church organist C. L. Boxberg provides an explanation of an engraving of its façade, in which he describes some thirty-two separate items, including suns, angels, wings, and the various sounds they made. For a facsimile and translation see Mary Murrell Faulkner, *C. L. Boxberg's 1704 Description of Casparini's Sun Organ in Görlitz: Translation and Commentary* (Saarbrücken: VDM Verlag Dr. Müller, 2009).

9. OBH, 20. Although two Cymbelstern may seem redundant, such pairs can also be found in seven other organs associated with Bach: see OBH, 25, 31, 36, 37, 113, 117, and 130. A connection between this stop and angels can also be found on some Spanish organs: Cordoba Cathedral, for example, where the revolving wheels appear to be activated by angels blowing on them. See Edward L. Stauf and Christian Ahrens, "Zimbelstern/Cymbelstern," *The Organ: An Encyclopedia*, edited by Douglas E. Bush and Richard Kassel (New York: Routledge, 2006), 653.

10. "Ubi sunt gaudia, nirgends mehr denn da! Da die Engel singen, o nova cantica, und die Schellen klingen, in Regis curia: eia wären wir da."

11. Vogelgesang stops could be found on a number of instruments during Bach's day, including those at the St. Thomas and St. Nicholas Churches in Leipzig as well as organs in Görlitz, Gotha, Halle, Hamburg, and Mühlhausen: see OBH, 27, 29, 31, 36, and 69. Many of these organs also had carved birds on their cases: for example, the Lange organ at St. Nicholas Church in Leipzig.

12. Christian Flottwell, *Ein wolgerührtes Orgel-Werck, als eine Anreitzung zur Frucht des Geistes . . . bey Einweihung der neün Orgel in der Kneiphöfischen Thum-Kirchen in öffentlicher Predigt vorgestellet* (Königsberg: Stelter, 1721), 27: "Last euch demnach, Ihr Meine Liebsten / durch dieses neu=erbaute Orgel=Werk zur heiligen Andacht in eurem Gottesdienst auffmuntern / daß ihr in dem Heiligthum des Herrn nicht wie die stummen Blöcke sitzet, sondern, wie ihr einen Vogel=Sang in unserer Orgel höret, euch also in die Höhe schwinget/vom Irdischen loß reisset, und die himmlische Music anstimmet: Gloria in Excelsis Deo! Ehre sey Gott in der Höhe!"

possible, on a second or even a third balcony. With the tools and machinery available to organ builders of this time, such great elevation required significant amounts of labor, logistics, and engineering prowess; yet the earliest organs that Bach encountered were situated in this manner: the Stertzing organ in St. George Church in Eisenach and the Wender organ in the New Church in Arnstadt, for instance.[13] The organ of the Weimar Schloßkapelle is perhaps the most extreme example from Bach's career of a heavenward organ placement: rather than reaching toward the ceiling of the church, this organ was placed above it.[14] By no surprise, the ceiling was painted blue and the church was known as "Weg zur Himmelsburg" [Path to the Fortress of Heaven]. The upper ceiling above this organ was painted with clouds and angels, and though the Weimar court could hardly have seen the instrument well, hearing a chorale like "Vom Himmel hoch" on this instrument must have been especially meaningful.[15] Bach's Mülhausen congregation looked up to a three-manual organ that had a large winged angel at the very top, a number of smaller angels, a twelve-bell Cymbelstern and a 32' Untersatz, all of which contributed to its perception as a musical representation of Heaven.[16] The Leipzig instruments, outfitted with similar accoutrements, doubtless inspired similar reverence.[17] The smaller organ in St. Thomas Church, by virtue of its "swallow's nest" position high above the floor of the church and its decoration, was the most celestial of the Leipzig instruments: both of the winged doors from the original 1489 instrument were inscribed "Sanctus, Sanctus, Sanctus // Domine Deus Zebaoth," words which, as Isaiah reports, the six-winged Seraphim repeated over and over.[18] Bach seems to have understood this organ's iconic status from the outset of his Leipzig tenure: he likely used it at his first Christmas service, for the interpolations in the Magnificat in E-flat (BWV 243a), which begin with the opening verse of the chorale *Vom Himmel hoch:* "From Heaven above to earth I come, to bring good news to every home."[19]

13. See OBH, 21 and 10, respectively.

14. See OBH, 92.

15. As Christoph Wolff notes: "For the worshippers, music from the *Capelle* above the ceiling, enhanced by the 'echo tower' effect of its dazzling acoustics, would have been perceived as sounds descending from Heaven—corresponding to the ancient imagery of an angels' concert" (*Johann Sebastian Bach: The Learned Musician* [New York: Norton, 2000], 123).

16. See OBH, 73, for a description of the St Blasius organ.

17. See OBH, 48–51 on the Leipzig New Church, St. Nicholas Church, and University Church organs.

18. See OBH, 53–54.

19. OBH, 54. Obbligato organ parts were common in Christmas cantatas especially. Examples by J. F. Agricola, J. S. Bach (BWV 63), J. P. Kellner, C. G. Kleeberg, J. G. Krebs, J. J. Quantz, G. H. Stölzel. J. K. Wagner, and G. P. Weimar are discussed in Matthew Cron, *The Obbligato Organ Cantatas of Johann Sebastian Bach in the Context of 18th-Century Practice* (PhD diss., Brandeis University, 2004), 251–69.

A popular devotional book in Bach's library, written by pastor and theologian Heinrich Müller (1631–1675),[20] made equally explicit claims for the organ's heavenly pedigree. Müller's *Göttlicher Liebes-Flamme* (*Divine Flame of Love*), first printed in 1659,[21] contains an illustration that graphically represents Ephesians 5:19, a passage where Paul exhorts, "Sing and play to the Lord in your hearts," with singers and stringed instruments making figural music around an organ (see plate 2).[22] This emblem, from the end of chapter 25 ("On the salvation of the Righteous"), features, above the heart, angels who are also making music; and in the middle of this heavenly choir there is a parallel organ plus a harp.[23] The caption reads:

> From my heart, I praise you, because of you and your goodness.
> O wonderfully great God, delight my mind,
> The heavens praise you, I have Heaven here on earth when I praise you
> —thus one becomes like an angel.

20. See Robin A. Leaver, *Bachs theologische Bibliothek: Eine kritische Bibliographie* [Bach's Theological Library: A Critical Bibliography], vol. 1 of *Beiträge zur theologischen Bachforschung* (Neuhausen-Stuttgart: Hänssler, 1983), which lists those theological books listed in the *Specificatio* of the possessions of J. S. Bach at the time of his death. The most frequently found author in Bach's library is Martin Luther, followed by August Pfeiffer and then Heinrich Müller.

21. Müller's emblem book was very popular and was reprinted at least thirteen times: see Leaver, *Bachs theologische Bibliothek*, 152. A recent discussion of this work in relation to Bach's music can be found in Marcel Samuel Zwitser, *Gottliche Liebes-Flamme: De Lutherse leer van de Heilige Geest en haar invloed op Johann Sebastian Bach* [Divine Flame of Love: The Lutheran Doctrine of the Holy Spirit and Its Influence on Johann Sebastian Bach], with a summary in English (doctoral diss., University of Utrecht, 2012).

22. This particular engraving is from the 1724 edition: see Heinrich Müller, *Doct. Heinrich Müllers Weilan der Theologischen Facultät Seniorn, und Superintendenten in Rostock, vermehrter und durchgehends verbesserter himmlischer Liebes-Flamme, oder Göttliche Liebes-Flamme* (Nuremberg: Adelbulner, 1724), facing p. 758. The 1676 edition may be seen at http://diglib.hab.de/drucke/th-1851/start.htm.

23. According to a letter from 1655 written by Johann Erasmus Kindermann, organist of St. Egidien Church in Nuremburg, two weeks before his death, it is Christ who leads the heavenly choir from the organ: "God the Father is the Capellmeister, or leader, of all the choirs of musicians. God the Son, who sits at the right of the Father, leads from the basso continuo as the organist of heaven with everlasting joy and blessedness. He plays on the pedals with his feet and all his enemies stumble at his feet. And God the Holy Spirit is the sweet, gentle, and blessed wind who dries our tears, that we now happily praise his abilities with unspeakable joy." Cited in Hans Eggebrecht, "Zwei Nürnberger Orgel-Allegorien des 17. Jahrhunderts. Zum Figur-Begriff der Musica Poetica," *Musik und Kirche* 27 (1957), 172: "Gott der Vater ist des ganzen Chori Musici Capellmeister oder Führer. Gott der Sohn, der rechten der Vaters sitzt, der führet als der himmlische Organist den Bassum Continuum, als die immerwährende Freud und Seligkeit. Er tritt mit seinem Füßen das Pedal, und stößet alle seine Feinde zu seinen Füßen. Und Gott der heilige Geist, der ist der süße, sanfte und selige Wind, der unsre zeitlichen Tränen austrocknet, daß wir itzt mit unaussprechlichen Freuden jauchzen und fröhlich sein können."

Plate 2. Emblem from Heinrich Müller, *Göttlicher Liebes-Flamme*

Making clear the organ's role in both earthly and heavenly musicmaking, the emblem illustrates the relationship between the faithful and the musicians who perform on their behalf: even those who neither sing nor play an instrument nevertheless experience the music in their hearts. The attached poem clarifies the organ's role not only in representing Heaven but in the way that figural music prepares the righteous for eternal life.[24]

24. Similar sentiments are expressed in John Dryden's "A Song for St. Cecilia's Day," written in 1687 and set to music (as an "Ode for St. Cecilia's Day") by G. F. Handel in 1739. While Dryden's descriptions of many musical instruments involve the emotions and passions that they raise ("the trumpet's loud clangor that excites us to war, the soft complaining flute that discovers the woes of hopeless

Among German writers such ideas were a commonplace of devotional as well as theoretical literature. Michael Praetorius, for example, maintains in the second volume of his *Syntagma Musicum* (1618) that "we must all, as servants of the Lord, make music . . . and in a steady constant *Cantorei* . . . let us learn the art on earth, which we will use in Heaven."[25] Or Johann Friderich Walther, organist of the Garnison-Kirche in Berlin, who concludes his lengthy description of the newly-built 1726 Joachim Wagner organ as follows:

> Yes, may great God grant, as we unite all our voices with the sweet sound of the organ, that some day in blessed eternity we may be worthy to raise our voices with all the holy angels and chosen ones in a sacred and beautiful harmony, and to praise and glorify without end the Triune God, Father, Son and Holy Spirit.[26]

Prefaces to hymnals and chorale books, the perfect place to reinforce this point to a wide audience, likewise admonished the faithful to "learn to sing . . . so that when you get to Heaven the holy angel can soon observe you, call you, and take you to your heavenly seat."[27]

Sermons preached at the dedication of new or renovated organs repeated and often expanded these ideas for the benefit of those present at the inauguration of a number of significant instruments. The connection of church music with salvation, for example, is made explicit in Johann Leonhard Fröreißen's sermon for the new organ of the main

---

lovers, the sharp violins that proclaim jealous pangs and frantic indignation"), his description of the organ is limited to its relationship to Heaven: "But oh! what art can teach/What human voice can reach/The sacred organ's praise? Notes inspiring holy love/Notes that wing their heavenly ways/ To join the choirs above."

25. Cited in Eggebrecht, *Zwei Nürnberger Orgel-Allegorien*, 173n7: "Denn im Himmel müssen wir alle, der Herr sowohl als der Knecht, musiciren . . . und eine stetige immerwährende Cantorey halten . . . Laßt uns die Kunst lernen auf Erden, die wir im Himmel gebrauchen werden."

26. Johann Friderich Walther, *Die, In der Königl: Garnison-Kirche zu Berlin, befindliche Neue Orgel, wie selbige, nach ihrer äussern und innern Beschaffenheit erbauet, mit wenigem beschrieben, und Nebst einer kurtzen Vorrede, vom Gebrauch, Kunst und Vortreflichkeit der Orgeln, zum Druck übergeben / von Johann Friderich Walther, Organist und Collega der Berlinischen Garnison-Kirche und Schule* (Berlin: Müller, 1726): "Ja der grosse Gott verleihe, dass wie wir alle unsere Stimmen, mit dem lieblichen Schall der Orgeln vereinigen, wir auch würdig werden mögen, dereinst in der seeligen Ewigkeit, mit allen heiligen Engeln und Auserwehlten in einer heiligen und schönen Harmonie, unsere Stimmen zu erheben, und den Dreyeinigen Gott, Vater, Sohn und heiligen Geist, zu loben und zu preisen ohne Ende."

27. From the *Geistlicher Harffen-Klang*, a large hymnal published in Leipzig in 1679 by Johann Quirsfeld. Cited in Eggebrecht, *Zwei Nürnberger Orgel-Allegorien*, 173: "Lernet singen . . . wann ihr werdet in den Himmel kommen, so werden's die heiligen Engel bald an Euch merken und Euch heißen zu ihrem himmlischen Pult treten."

evangelical church in Straßburg; following the reading of Psalm 150, this sermon begins by noting, in Latin and German, that "music is a foretaste of eternal life."[28] Such an exalted role for music is also expressed in a sermon Johann Conrad Feuerlein preached at the dedication of the newly renovated organ at the St. Sebald Church in Nuremburg. This sermon (originally delivered in 1691 but not published until 1696, shortly after Johann Pachelbel became organist) describes the organ in terms everyone could understand, as a way of elucidating key concepts of Lutheran belief.

> Some people who understand the design of an organ say that it can be compared to the human body, which is led and directed by the mind. This comparison would run as follows:
>
> On the one side, the organ emits a sweet and beautiful sound with the help of a flow of air; this is to the organ what the mind and soul are to man. And in comparison, a person can perform well-sounding speaking with the help of the mind. For man, we have the lungs, for the organ the bellows; man has a windpipe and vocal chords, the organ has pipes; man, the teeth, the organ a keyboard; man, a tongue, the organ an organist who converts the thoughts into the music. Just as it is with speaking: the hearing thereof is pleasant when the thoughts are good. With that, I leave you to consider whether this is a good metaphor.
>
> But tell me, while we're comparing the organ to the human body, if a man becomes ill and weak from the ravage of sickness, what shall we do? Dear Christians, we shall do what is at all times necessary for the soul, for the prospering of man, and to the glory of God. And what is that? I will briefly explain it to you in the terms of the different registers of our renovated St. Sebald organ.[29]

Individual stops, Feuerlein goes on to note, can comfort the ill and weak, assuage the soul, even promote prosperity—all while glorifying God. His multiple descriptions include a number of memorable characterizations:

28. Johann Leonhard Fröreißen, *Christliche Predigt, Welche Bey der sogenannten Einweyhung der neuen Orgel in der Evangel: Haupt=Kirch zu Straßburg Sonntags den 16. Nov. 1749. gehalten worden von Johann Leonhard Fröreißen, Der Heil. Schrift D. und P. P. des Collegiat-Stiffts zu St. Thomas Canonico, E. E. Kirchen=Convents Praeside und Pastore Primario* (Straßburg: Pauschinger, 1749), 6.

29. Conrad Feuerlein, *In Dutiful Praise to God / (as expressed in the words of Psalm 150, v. 4) / "Praise the Lord with Strings and Pipes!"/ the year of our Lord, 1691 / St. Sebald Day / on the occasion of the solemn dedication / of the renovations and improvements of the / great organ in the Senior Church and Bishop's Seat / St. Sebald Nürnberg / an afternoon service of Vespers / with sermon by Pastor Conrad Feuerlein / and blessing of all the above-mentioned ranks of pipes, in relevant records / which sermon now freely published by / permission of the author / Wolfgang Moritz Endter, publisher, 1696*, translated by John E. Rimbach (Spokane, Wash.: Rimbach, 1996), 15–17.

Principal: reminds you of the principal act of being acceptable and justified to God in order "to achieve santification in the further life."

Grobgedackt: a deep and coarse voice that "comes directly to mind when we are threatened by sin and the deep, rasping drone of fear begins in our heart."

Oktave: "which goes into the higher pitches and reminds you, dear Christians, of the songs which we will one day, together with the angels, sing out in the heavenly chorus in the praise of God."

Quint: a strong and forceful stop which reminds you in times of need and difficulty to "cry out with your whole heart, not doubting, that your cries will pierce through the dark clouds."[30]

Such allegorical descriptions are of course not meant to be taken too literally; instead, their function is to portray the organ as an embodiment of a good Christian: the instrument possesses the most desirable physical and intellectual attributes of man himself and reminds one of proper Christian conduct. Those who are unable to sing or play can do so vicariously through the organ, while those who are physically ill can have their souls uplifted through hearing it. Concluding this sermon, Feuerlein draws a parallel between the renovated instrument and the newly inspired congregation:

> Yes, you too, my Christian friends, who have been taught these things, let your heart and voice daily be filled with the praise and honor of God. Think of it! You are a renovated creation of God [*ein renovirtes Werk Gottes*], renewed to his glory, through the Spirit of his grace which carried this to fulfillment in you.[31]

A more striking vision of the organ's power can be found in a pair of 1721 sermons delivered at the dedication of a new organ by Johann Joshua Mosengel and members of the Casparini family for Königsberg Cathedral, which replaced an instrument from 1587 (see plate 3).[32] These sermons, by Pastor Christian Masecovius and Deacon M. Christian Flottwell for morning and vespers dedication services, respectively, describe the new three-manual instrument of some five thousand pipes as having a voice loud enough for God to hear it. This remarkable organ, they maintained, could also guide, inspire, uplift, and comfort the congregation while providing a "right and loud teaching voice." The following passage places great emphasis on one particular lesson:

> I see carved angels on the organ with trumpets in their hands. I hear under these the rumbling bass-voice sounding, by which I picture [the organ] as a teaching voice of the future universal resurrection on Judgement Day. The time comes when Jesus

30. Feuerlien, *In Dutiful Praise of God*, 17–19. Quotations are original though uncredited.

31. *Ibid.*, 19.

32. The Kneiphoff church was the Protestant cathedral of Königsberg (now Kaliningrad) from 1523 until 1946.

> will appear for judgement not with carved angels from the hand of a mortal master but with throne [angels] and dominion angels, which his omnipotence created at the beginning of the world. The son of man shall come in his glory and all the holy angels with him. (*Matthew 25:31*) The time comes when the heavenly master over all masters of the entire earth will enter, where all the dead rest, like an organ pedal with the foot of his Godly omnipotence. The time will come when first a bass voice will crack like thunder: the dead will rise up and come for judgment and all the sleeping will be woken with a loud voice.
>
> The hour is coming, and is now, when the dead shall hear the voice of the Son of God: and they that hear shall live. (*John 5:25*) Ah, how the organ pipes will sound in countless multitudes! How the *Vox tremulans* will be heard by many of the godless with frightful tremors from mountains and rocks: fall on us, and hide us from the face of Him that sitteth on the throne, and from the wrath of the Lamb. (*Rev. 6:16*) On the contrary, the *Vox humana* will be heard in all loving tones by so many thousands of the chosen at the holy sight of the universal judge in the friendliest human form: Amen, even so, come Lord Jesus. (*Rev. 22:20*) And in such a manner *can our organ also be a teaching voice whereby the account of its nature will then be completely revealed.*[33]

This vision of the last judgement, predicated in part on the Mosengel organ's decoration and the sounds of particular registers, enlarges considerably the ideological range

33. Christian Masecovius, *Die Kneiphöffsche laute Orgel-Stimme, welche in diesem 1721sten Jahr am XIV. Sonntage nach Trinitatis . . . zur Inauguration dieses neün Orgel-Wercks . . . in der Vormittags Predigt vorgetragen . . . Christian Masecovius* (Königsberg: Stelter, 1721), 23–4: "Ich sehe geschnitze Engel an der Orgel mit Posaunen in ihren Händen. Ich höre unter selbigen die drähnende Baß-Stimme erthönen / wodurch ich sie abbilde als eine lehrende Stimme künfftiger allgemeinen Aufferstehung zum Jüngsten Gericht. Es kommt die Zeit / daß Jesus zum Gericht erschienen werde nicht mit geschnitzten Engeln von der Hand eines sterblichen Meisters / sondern mit Thronen und Herrschafften / welche seine Allmacht im Anfang der Welt erschaffen. Des Menschen Sohn wird kommen in seiner Herrlichkeit / und alle heilige Engel mit ihm. *Matth. XXV, 31.* Es kommt die Zeit / da der himmlische Meister über alle Meister die ganze Erde / wo alle Todten ruhen / wie ein Orgel=Pedal mit dem Fuß seiner Göttlichen Allmacht betreten wird / es kommt die Zeit / da erst die Baß=Stimme wie ein Donner erknallen wird: Stehet auf ihre Todten / und kommt vor Gericht / und alle Schlaffende mit einer lauten Stimme auffwecken. Es kommt die Stunde / und ist schon ietzt / daß die Todten werden die Stimme des Sohnes Gottes hören / und die sie hören werden / die werden leben. *Joh. V, 25.* Ach wie werden als denn in unzähliger Menge die Orgel-Pfeiffen erklingen! Wie wird die *Vox tremulans* aus vielen Gottlosen mit erschrecklichem Zittern die Stimme von sich hören lassen zu den Bergen und Felsen: Fallet auf uns und verberget uns vor dem Angesicht des / der auf dem Stuhl sitzt / und vor dem Zorn des Lammes. *Apoc. VI: 16.* Im Gegentheil die Vox humana wird aus so viel tausend Auserwehlten über den seeligen Anblick des allgemeinen Richters in der freundlichsten Menschlichen Gestalt im allerlieblichsten Freuden=Thon sich vernehmen lassen: Amen ja komm Herr Jesu / *Apoc. XXII, 20.* Und auf solche Art kan unsere Orgel auch eine lehrende Stime seyn / wodurch denn gäntzlich die Beschreibung ihres Wesens *absolviret* wird" (emphasis added).

Plate 3. Mosengel organ in Königsberg Cathedral

of the instrument: representing all facets of the Almighty, this thunderous organ could conjure the terrors of hell just as easily as its more beautiful sounds could summon Heaven's peace.[34]

The libretti of cantatas with obbligato organ are a particularly rich source of literary and theological arguments for this view of the organ as a kind of musical gateway to Heaven. In addition to the eighteen Bach cantatas with concerted organ movements,

34. Such views of the organ as part of the celestial harmony are found in a number of seventeenth-century sources and are discussed in Hans Davidsson, "The Organ in Seventeenth-Century Cosmology," in *The Organ as a Mirror of Its Time: Northern European Reflections, 1610–2000*, edited by Kerala Snyder (Oxford: Oxford University Press, 2002), 78–91. The idea is also found in eighteenth-century sources, including poetry written by the organist, composer, and cantor Theodor Reinholdt for the newly built Gottfried Silbermann organ in the Frauenkirche in Dresden. See Theodor Christlieb Reinholdt, *Einige zur Musik gehörige poetische Gedanken bei Gelegenheit der schönen neuen in der Frauenkirche in Dresden verfertigten Orgel* (Dresden: Hilschern, 1736), 8–9.

there are at least 130 other such cantatas from the eighteenth century, including thirty-five extant works by Gottfried Heinrich Stölzel as well as works by Wilhelm Friedemann and Carl Philipp Emmanuel Bach, Georg Philipp Telemann, various Bach students (Agricola, Doles, Homilius, J. P. Kellner, and Trier), and their pupils (Naumann, Reichardt, Tag, and Türk).[35] The majority of these obbligato organ movements contain texts that refer specifically to different aspects of Heaven, including entry into Heaven, singing in heavenly choirs, the comfort of Heaven, its light, wind, even rain and thunder.

An emphasis on hymn singing as preparation for the heavenly choir is found in numerous cantatas by Telemann and Stölzel.[36] One particularly good example can be found in Telemann's cantata *Der Himmel ist offen*, TWV 1:296, written for Ascension Day, 1732. Its text, from Erdmann Neumeister's *Geistliche Cantaten* (1702),[37] may begin with Jesus's ascension, though its focus is very much on that of the congregation: like the sermon texts quoted above, it identifies how one can enter Heaven and sing with the heavenly choir.

1. Tutti (SATB, 2 ob, 2 vln, va, bc)	
Der Himmel ist offen!	The heavens have opened.
2. Recitative (B, bc)	
Mein Jesus fährt hinauf,	My Jesus ascends,
die Stätte zu bereiten,	to prepare the place,

35. For an inventory of these works including title, occasion, instrumentation, movements with obbligato organ, and sources, see the appendix of Cron, *The Obbligato Organ Cantatas*. This dissertation also includes chapters discussing the function, text, symbolism, and musical characteristics of this repertoire with many musical examples and several specific case studies.

36. Stölzel is known to Bach scholars not only through the aria "Bist du bei mir" (from Stölzel's opera *Diademate*), which Bach copied into the notebook for his wife Anna Magdalena, but also through recent research by Tatiana Schabalina, Peter Wollny, Marc-Roderich Pfau, and Andreas Glöckner, who have shown that Bach also performed a number of Stölzel's church works in the 1730s, including the passion oratorio *Ein Lämmlein geht und trägt die Schuld* in 1734. See Marc-Roderich Pfau, "Ein unbekanntes Leipziger Kantatetextheft aus der Jahr 1735-Neues zum Thema Bach and Stölzel," *Bach-Jahrbuch* 94 (2008): 99–122; Peter Wollny, "'Bekennen will ich seinen Namen': Authentizität, Bestimmung und Kontext der Aria BWV 200. Anmerkungen zu Johann Sebastian Bachs Rezeption von Werken Gottfried Heinrich Stölzels," *Bach-Jahrbuch* 94 (2008): 123–58; and Andreas Glöckner, "Ein weiterer Kantatenjahrgang Gottfried Heinrich Stölzels in Bachs Aufführungsrepertoire?" *Bach-Jahrbuch* 95 (2009): 95–115. See also Christoph Wolff, "Under the Spell of Opera? Bach's Oratorio Trilogy," *Bach Perspectives 8: J. S. Bach and the Oratorio Tradition*, edited by Daniel R. Melamed (Urbana: University of Illinois Press, 2011), 3.

37. This publication's texts are also included in Erdmann Neumeister, *Fünffache Kirchen-Andachten* (1716), 703.

die wir nach diesen Zeiten	where after these times
und auf vollbrachten lauf	and at completed course
bey Ihm bewohnen sollen.	we shall dwell with him.
Wer sollte nun den Sitz der Eitelkeiten	Who shall now not want to abandon
mit Freuden nicht verlaßen wollen?	with joy the seat of vanities?

3. Aria (S, 2 vln, va, calcedono concertante, bc)

Gute Nacht, du schnödes Wesen	Good night, you wretched creature
das die Welt zur Lust erlesen!	that this world chose for amusement,
denn der Himmel steht mir an.	for now Heaven stands before me.
Den nur will ich erkießen,	That is what I want to choose;
Jesus hat den Weg gewießen	Jesus has shown the way
und die Pforten aufgethan.	and opened the gates.

4. Recit. (T, bc)

Hier muß ich nur ein Pilgrim sein,	Here must I only a pilgrim be,
Mein Bürger-Recht und Wandel ist dort oben,	my citizen rights and dealings are up there,
Wo alle Seraphim den höchsten ewig loben.	where all the seraphim eternally praise the highest one.
Da ist mein Vaterland,	There is my fatherland,
da sehn' ich mich hinein.	up there I long to be.
Welt, weg, du bist mir unbekannt;	World, away, you are unknown to me:
ich trachte nur nach dem das droben,	I try only for that [place] above,
da ist mein höchstes Gut,	which is my greatest good,
und das macht rechten Muth,	and rightly encourages,
diß kan mein Herz unfehlbar hoffen.	for this can my heart hope without fail.

5. Tutti 1 repeated

6. Aria. (B, 2 ob, 2 vln, va, bc)

Mir grauet, Welt, vor deinem Thun,	I am terrified, world, by your ways,
und so viel Ärgernüssen.	and by so many annoyances.
Ich will in Jesu Schooße ruhn,	I want to rest on Jesus's bosom
und seine Schönheit küssen.	and embrace his radiance.
Ach komm, mein Jesu, komm nur bald,	Ah come, my Jesus, only come soon,
mein Schatz, mein Trost, mein Aufenthalt,	my treasure, my comfort, my abode,
und führe mich zum Himmel.	and lead me to Heaven.

7. Aria (A, 2 vln, va, org obl, bc)

Da will ich mit der Engel-Schaar	There will I with the host of angels
dein heilig Lob besingen,	sing your holy praise,
nicht Zehn- nicht Hundert-Tausend Jahr	not for ten thousand nor a hundred thousand years

soll diß vor dir erklingen.	should this resound before you.
Nein, allezeit und ohne Zeit,	No, for all time and without time,
von Ewigkeit zu Ewigkeit,	from eternity to eternity,
soll diß Gepränge währen.	shall this majesty last.
8. Chorale (SATB, 2 ob, 2 vln, va, org, bc)	
Unaussprechlich Schöne singet Gottes auser-	With unspeakable beauty sings God's
wähltes Schaar, heilig, heilig, heilig,	chosen choir: Holy, Holy, Holy,
klinget in dem Himmel innen dar.	resounding in Heaven itself.
Welt bei dir ist Spott und Hohn,	World, with you is derision and mockery
und ein steter Jammer-Ton,	and a constant sound of sorrow,
aber dort ist aller Zeit	but [up] there is for all time
Friede, Freud und Seeligkeit.	peace, joy, and blessedness.

Following the opening declaration, this first-person libretto contrasts a wretched earthly existence with eternal life in Heaven. Though Neumeister's original text ends with two verses of a chorale, Telemann sets these two verses as separate arias and adds a new chorale verse at the end. These two arias make for the sharpest contrast between earthly and heavenly existence in the work. The first—a somber A-minor Largo scored for bass, muted oboes, muted strings, and continuo—expresses the vexations of earthly existence while imploring Christ to illuminate the path to Heaven. A joyful A-major alto aria follows, accompanied by oboes, strings, and *organo concertante* (see examples 1 and 2).

The alto aria is the first to feature solo organ in a prominent treble (right-hand) melody; its subject matter, the eternal praise of God in song, brings about the heavenly bliss that the final chorale celebrates. From the very first note of the organ solo, we perceive a shift from minor to major, from the tribulations of earthly existence to the delight of singing for eternty with the heavenly choir. The contrast is further heightened by a change in figuration, from the descending sighs of the bass aria to an upward skipping pattern that permeates the concertante organ part in the alto aria. Telemann's strategy, of saving the obbligato organ for precisely that moment in his cantata where a heavenward ascent is assured not only for Jesus but for all the faithful, would not have been lost on members of his congregation, who were accustomed to such associations from abundant visual, homiletic, and literary reminders.

Stölzel emphasized this point repeatedly in cantatas for which he wrote both music and text. A student of theology at the University of Leipzig from 1707 to 1710, Stölzel made a name for himself as both composer and poet, earning praise from Ernst Ludwig Gerber (among others), who notes in his *Historisch-Biographisches Lexicon der Tonkünstler* (1792) that "younger composers have made good use of what Stölzel did

Ex. 1. G. P. Telemann, *Der Himmel ist offen*, mvt. 6, mm. 20–29

Ex. 1. Continued

Ex. 2. G. P. Telemann, *Der Himmel ist offen*, mvt. 7, mm. 1–3, 19–23

before them. But Stölzel has also accomplished a number of things that I have not found in any newer work. His wit in expressing his texts musically is inexhaustible."[38] Stölzel wrote the libretti for four of his ten cantata cycles, meaning that he chose (likely in consultation with a supervising pastor) the Bible verse or *dictum*, selected the final chorale and its verses, and wrote all the poetry for intervening recitatives and arias.[39] Two other of his cycles, *Gott-geheiligtes Singen und Spielen des Friedensteinischen Zions* and *Das Saiten-Spiel des Hertzens*,[40] allude in their titles to the idea of "singing and playing in one's heart," a common theme in this repertory. Stölzel's cantata *Singet und spielet dem Herrn in euren Herzen*, from one of his own collections of poetry,[41] highlights this idea within a cantata that calls for obbligato organ in several movements: the opening chorus, a soprano-tenor duetto and a bass aria. Its first three movements, which rely on a familiar passage from Ephesians 5:19, speak directly to the congregation:

1. Tutti (SATB, 2 vln, va, 'Organo' obl)

Singet und spielet dem Herrn in euren Herzen.	Sing and play to the Lord in your hearts.

2. Recit. (SAT, bc)

[S] Das Herz muß deine Zunge rühren, wann dein Gesang zu Gottes Herze dringen soll,	The heart must lead your tongue, if your song is to penetrate God's heart.

38. Quoted in Manfred Fechner, ed., *Gottfried Heinrich Stölzel, 1690–1749. Weihnachtskantaten: für den Hof Schwarzburg-Sondershausen (aus den Doppeljahrgang 1736/37 und 1739)*, translated by Stephanie Wollny (Leipzig: Hofmeister, 2006): xi, xiv. Gerber grew up in Sondershausen, where his father performed the organ parts for many cantatas cycles that were commissioned from Stölzel. A 1765 memorandum on the "Improvement of Sacred Music in Rural Communities" [*Verbeßerung der Kirchen Musik auf dem Lande*] likewise notes that Stölzel's cantatas "have texts full of spirit and spiritual life, and what is said by the words is also expressed by the sweetest harmonies as both come from the same author." In the introduction to the printed text of Stölzel's first cantata cycle, the senior pastor of the Gotha Court, A. G. Ludwig, links the composer to the psalmists by referring to him as a "qualified and renowned Asaph." Johann Oswald Knauer, *Gott-geheiligtes Singen und Spielen des Friedensteinischen Zions* (Gotha, 1721), v–vi.

39. In his autobiography published in Johann Mattheson's *Grundlage einer Ehren-Pforte* (1740), Stölzel writes that he always connected his "proper professional work as a musician . . . [with] that of a poet."

40. The librettist of the first of these cycles, set by Stölzel for services at the Gotha Court Chapel in 1721–22, was Johann Oswald Knauer, a pastor in Schleiz whose daughter Stölzel married in 1719. The second cycle's texts, set by Stölzel in 1724–25, came from Benjamin Schmolck. This cycle (*Die Saiten-Spiel des Hertzens*) was partially, or perhaps completely, performed by J. S. Bach in Leipzig from the First Sunday after Trinity 1735 to Trinity Sunday 1736.

41. *Das Gläubige Herz* (1728–29), published in Gotha in 1761. Stölzel recycled this text in a new musical setting for a Thanksgiving Concert sometime after 1730. See Fritz Hennenberg, *Das Kantatenschaffen Gottfried Heinrich Stölzels*, vol. 8 of *Beiträge zur musikwissenschaftlichen Forschung in DDR*, (Leipzig: Deutscher Verlag für Musik, 1976), 130.

[A] Das Herz muß dir die Hände rühren	The heart must lead the hands,
sonst klinget die Instrumenten Klang,	since instrumental sound alone,
niehmahls in Gottes Ohren wohl.	won't please God's ears.
[T] Dein Spielen und dein singen wird	Your singing and your playing
deinen Gott kein süßes Opffer seyn,	will be to God no sweet offering,
du must denn solches ihm allein,	you must then to him alone,
auf dem Altar des Hertzens bringen.	to the altar bring your heart.
3. 'Duetto' (ST, 2 vln, org)	
Man singt und spielet nur dem Herren	One sings and plays to the Lord only
wenn Mund und Herz zusammen stimmt.	when mouth and heart are in agreement.
Wann auch bei deinen Lobgesängen	Just as your song of praise
die lieblichsten Accorde klängen,	makes the loveliest chords resound,
so bleiben sie ein wüstes plerren,	it remains a wild bawling,
wann man das Herz von solchen nimmt	when one sings without heart.

The message here, that body and soul must act together in praise of God, posits musical harmony as a representation of the harmonious communion between God and the faithful. An obbligato organ lends its voice quite naturally to such sentiments, providing a kind of metaphorical bridge between the congregation and the Almighty. Thus the instrument that leads the congregation in hymn singing also asserts itself in figural music, to reinforce references to Heaven found in the texts of many church cantatas from the early eighteenth century.

A number of Bach's obbligato organ cantatas may be cited in this regard. The struggle to reach the Kingdom of Heaven is the main focus of BWV 146, whose opening chorus quotes Acts 14:22: "We must through much tribulation enter into the kingdom of God" (Wir müssen durch viel Trübsal in das Reich Gottes eingehen). Preceding this chorus is a sinfonia for concertante organ, oboes, and strings. The Leipzig congregation had already heard several opening sinfonias in Bach's cantatas, particularly in reperformances of pre-Leipzig works (BWV 4, 12, 18, 21, 31, and 182) but also in new works (BWV 42 and 52).[42] But as far as we know, Cantata 146 was likely the first Leipzig work with an opening sinfonia featuring solo organ.[43] Though Bach's incorporation of

42. Instrumental sinfonias would have also been heard after the sermon to open the second parts of BWV 75 and 76.

43. Since the original score and parts of this cantata have not survived, its dating to Jubilate Sunday 1726 is not definitive; its first performance may have been in 1728. If BWV 146 was performed in 1726, it would have begun a series of obbligato organ cantatas from Sundays in Pentecost during that year. Bach's Leipzig congregation would have already heard an obbligato organ in one of his earlier works: in *Wachet, betet, betet wachet*, BWV 70, in November 1724. This cantata for the end of the church year is concerned with the day of judgement and prominently uses a solo trumpet to reinforce this

violinistic elements—*bariolage*, for example, in the organ obbligato—may have struck attentive listeners as unusual, in context this movement's more traditional figuration is actually more surprising, serving to throw into high relief the organ obbligato. In an interlude at the middle of the movement (see example 3), Bach mimics the style of interludes between the lines of his cantional-style organ chorales (for example, BWV 715 or 722) in passagework that takes advantage of the wide range of the organ with scalar passages and various types of figuration. Bach's contemporaries would have heard such interludes regularly in hymn singing, and in order to participate fully, they had to listen actively and respond from line to line. And yet, even for those listeners who were also familiar with concerto form, an interlude such as this—in the middle of a concerted sinfonia—was an unprecedented intrusion in a cantata sinfonia.[44] Even among Vivaldi's many concertos, a passage with a similar character and placement cannot be found.[45] From a modern perspective, by contrast, this passage in BWV 146/1 seems like a mid-movement cadenza, a concerto-style "event" that we have come to expect near the end of a movement in this genre.

The organ part in the ensuing chorus may have also puzzled Bach's congregation: the organ enters at the end of the first choral statement in short phrases that lack obvious connection to what preceded them. An allusion to the style of the ornamented chorale prelude seems clear, although as the movement progresses, the organ obbligato becomes more rhapsodic and chromatic; it provides a kind of foil for the choral phrases by overlapping with its text, which emphasizes the suffering necessary before entry into Heaven. Throughout this movement the organ appears to be leading the music in odd directions, few of which lead to stable resolutions. While some of the more sophisticated members of Bach's congregation might have acknowledged the debt to Vivaldi in the opening and closing unison ritornellos, the presence of a choir further complicates the issue; this style of solo keyboard writing is found, moreover, in only one other place in Bach's numerous concerto transcriptions for keyboard and organ.[46]

---

association. Its alto aria with obbligato organ is introduced by a bass recitative that assures us not to be afraid at the last judgement. The aria itself expresses the joyful anticipation of being in Heaven.

44. The only comparable work from Bach is his Prelude and Fugue in A minor, BWV 894, whose interludes function in the same manner. In mm. 53–63 of this work, there are three non-thematic interludes that separate short phrases of thematic material and lead from one to the next.

45. The frequency, nature, and dissemination of Vivaldi's concerto cadenzas are discussed in Karl Heller, *Vivaldi: The Red Priest of Venice*, translated by David Marinelli (Portland, Ore.: Amadeus, 1997), 72–75.

46. The embellishments Bach added in his concerto transcriptions for keyboard and organ have a more limited range and employ repeated patterns of music material. But as Peter Williams notes about the *passagi* in the middle movement 'Recitative' of BWV 594: "[This] movement is not only

Ex. 3. J. S. Bach, *Wir müssen durch viel Trübsal*, BWV 146/1, mm. 109–12

This movement, with its seeming disconnect between elaborate organ writing and choral declamation, dramatizes the believer's arduous journey toward Heaven. The opening sinfonia, in retrospect, makes for a portentous beginning to the whole, with the solo organ functioning as the most prominent voice in the musical drama and as a kind of metaphorical sounding board to the next world.

In both of these movements, the right-hand organ obbligato is set in the lower register, frequently descending beneath the bass line by as much as an octave. The later harpsichord version of these movements (BWV 1052/1–2), which transposes the obbligato up an octave, makes clear that the right-hand part of the organ versions needs to be played on a 4´ rather than an 8´ registration. (This would be consistent with Feuerlein's argument cited above, that the "high-sounding Octav . . . reminds you, O Christ, of the songs that we will one day intone in the sublime choir in praise of God and will sing eternally with the angels.") The effect, in performances of Cantata 146, is an obbligato that soars above the musical texture, reminding listeners that Heaven awaits those who, through faith, endure life's tribulations. A similar effect is achieved in the third movement, an upbeat alto aria with an organ obbligato in the style of a solo violin (this time, at unison pitch) whose text affirms Heaven as a destination for those who reject Sodom and worldly idleness.

Such a progression—from despair to peace, earthly to heavenly existence—can be found in numerous other Bach cantatas that call for obbligato organ: throughout *Ich*

---

unique in the concerto corpus of Vivaldi . . . but no more than faintly resembles textures in other Bach works, such as the opening of the G minor Fantasia." See Peter Williams, *The Organ Music of J. S. Bach*, 2nd ed. (Cambridge: Cambridge University Press, 2003), 306.

geh und suche mit Verlangen, BWV 49, for instance.[47] Knowledge of the afterlife, to this way of thinking, offers *Trost* (comfort or solace) for this life's tribulations as well as joyful anticipation.[48] From his first essays in the genre, Bach instinctively grasped the comfort that could be conveyed wordlessly—via an elaborate organ part—in cantatas whose libretti addressed these themes. The Mühlhausen cantata *Gott ist mein König*, BWV 71, is a case in point: its tenor/soprano duet is adorned by an organ obbligato that seems to respond directly to the troubled tenor. To one contemplating death, comfort comes here on two simultaneous fronts: a flowing organ obbligato and a soprano chorale (see example 4). Leipzig obbligato organ cantatas tend to treat the organ more expansively, frequently with lively concerto-like writing. *Gott soll allein mein Herze haben*, BWV 169, for example, features three movements with concerted obbligatos, including two arias that make much of the idea that God, not our earthly existence or desires, is the source of all goodness. For a congregation that felt keenly the frustrations of life on earth, such music expressed the solace and joy of salvation.

Occasionally, Bach went beyond the norms established by his colleagues and used starkly opposed styles of obbligato writing for the organ within the same cantata, as a way of underlining its libretto's progession of thought. Such is the case with *Vergnügte Ruh, beliebte Seelenlust*, BWV 170, from July 1726. Following an opening aria ("Vergnügte Ruh!") whose text locates true contentment in Heaven and a recitative that laments how far man has strayed from God, the second aria—one of two featuring obbligato organ—expresses profound pity for the wayward hearts who take pleasure in ven-

47. See also the opening alto aria of *Komm, du süße Todesstunde*, BWV 161, in which the voice welcomes death as the organ plays the chorale *Herzlich tut mich verlangen* on a sesquialtera stop with a chordal accompaniment, in the manner of a chorale prelude; or the alto aria from Cantata 27 (*Wer weiß, wie nahe mir mein Ende?*), which welcomes the hour of death, though its scoring for oboe da caccia and either obbligato harpsichord or organ has more the character of an accompaniment than a prominent solo part.

48. The theme of *Trost* is found in obbligato organ cantatas by Agricola, W. F. Bach, Doles, Fehre, Gruner, Homilius, König, Stölzel, Tag, and Telemann: see Cron, *Obbligato Organ Cantatas*, 269–72. The singing of hymns and psalms was not only preparation for singing in Heaven and the afterlife but was also considered a source of solace on earth. The title pages of several eighteenth-century hymnals refer to "Trost-reiche" hymns and psalms: *Neu eingerichtetes und vermehrtes Essendisches Gesang-Buch: darinnen 632 auserlesene Geist-Lehr und trost-reiche Liede . . .* 11th ed. (Essen, 1766); *Geistliche Hertzens-Music oder neuvermehrtes Schleusingisches Gesangbuch, darinen Martin Luther und anderer Evangelischer Männer Geist- und Trost-reiche Psalmen und Lieder* (Schleusingen, 1748); and *Vollständiges Marburger Gesang-Buch: Zur uebung der Gottseligkeit; Worinnen 615 auserlesene Trost-reiche Psalmen und Gesänge hn. D. Martin Luthers und anderer Gottseliger Lehrer* (Marburg and Frankfurt am Main, 1770, 1781, 1790).

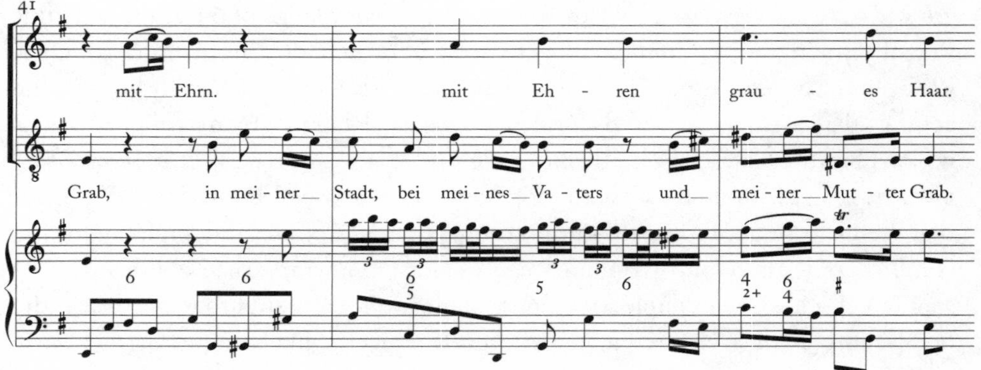

Ex. 4. J. S. Bach, *Gott ist mein König*, BWV 71/2, mm. 34–37

geance and pain and insolently flout God's will. Musically, this aria ("Wie jammern mich") represents a world that has been turned upside down: the violins and viola play a unison *bassett* line while the organ supplies two craggy independent melodic lines that hover over the voice and strings, all without continuo support. In sharp contrast to the pastoral nature of the opening movement, this highly chromatic aria wanders with little resolution, as the alto recounts with horror mankind's many perversions. Relief from the serpentine nature of the obbligato organ and alto parts comes only at the words "Rach und Haß" ("vengeance and hate"), as all three lines suddenly take flight in cascades of rising and falling 32nd notes (see example 5). The final aria, by contrast, is a more traditional ritornello-based work whose text ("Mir ekelt mehr zu leben") rejects earthly existence in favor of life in Heaven with Jesus. Its lively melody and joyous *Affekt* are premised on the hope of salvation, which is represented here, at least in part, by an organ obbligato that provides an elaboration of a swinging melody shared by first violin and oboe d'amore.

In the case of one exceptional work that was adapted to multiple purposes over nearly a decade, Bach's addition of organ obbligato served to recontextualize a cantata libretto. The surviving versions of *Höchsterwünschtes Freudenfest*, BWV 194, comprise these sequences of movements as performed in Leipzig in the following years:

Ex. 5. J. S. Bach, *Vergnügte Ruh, beliebte Seelenlust*, BWV 170/3, mm. 20–21

1723, 1724, and 1731 versions	1726 version
Part 1	
1. Chorus: *Höchsterwünschtes Freudenfest*	1. Chorale (= No. 12) *Sprich Ja zu meinen Taten*
2. Bass Recit: *Unendlich großer Gott, ach wende dich*	2. Bass Recit: *Unendlich großer Gott, ach wende dich*
3. Bass Aria: *Was des Höchsten Glanz erfüllt*	3. Bass Aria: *Was des Höchsten Glanz erfüllt*
4. Soprano Recit: *Wie könnte dir, du höchstes Angesicht*	4. Soprano Recit: *Wie könnte dir, du höchstes Angesicht*
5. Soprano Aria: *Hilf, Gott, dass es uns gelingt*	5. Soprano Aria: *Hilf, Gott, dass es uns gelingt*
6. Chorale: *Heilger Geist ins Himmels Throne*	6. Tenor Recit. (= No. 7): *Ihr Heiligen, erfreuet euch*
	7. Soprano and Bass Duet (= No. 10): *O wie wohl ist uns geschehn*
Part 2	
7. Tenor Recit: *Ihr Heiligen, erfreuet euch*	
8. Tenor Aria: *Des Höchsten Gegenwart allein*	
9. Bass and Soprano Recit: *Kann wohl ein Mensch zu Gott im Himmel steigen*	
10. Soprano and Bass Duet: *O wie wohl ist uns geschehn*	
11. Bass Recit: *Wohlan demnach, du heilige Gemei*	
12. Chorale: *Sprich Ja zu meinen Taten*	

With its origins in a secular cantata from the Cöthen years for which only fragments survive, *Höchsterwünschtes Freudenfest* first accompanied the 1723 consecration of the renovated sanctuary of the church in Störmthal, which boasted a new Hildebrandt organ. In 1724 Bach reprised the work with slight changes for the Leipzig churches; in 1726 he returned to the work again but this time in a shortened version with obbligato organ taking the place of other instrumental obbligatos in two arias. A 1731 performance of the 1724 version is the last recorded performance during his lifetime.[49]

An explanation for the organ obbligatos in the 1726 version can be found by comparing the texts of the two versions of this cantata. The longer version, created for the rededication of a church and the inaugural of its new organ, asks for God's blessing of a newly erected sanctuary on earth; while the shorter version, as presented in

49. See Alfred Dürr, *The Cantatas of J. S. Bach: With Their Librettos in German-English Parallel Text*, revised and translated by Richard D. P. Jones (Oxford: Oxford University Press, 2005), 719.

Leipzig during a season that included a number of obbligato organ cantatas,[50] places more emphasis on personal faith and salvation but also on the joyful light of God's countenance. Their respective opening movements, which diverge significantly in both theology and musical style, set the tone for each. The festive chorus *Höchsterwünschtes Freudenfest*, cast in the style of a French overture, exults that the "Lord, to his Glory, allows us to celebrate the newly-erected sanctuary," while the 1726 cantata begins with a simple hymn, "Wake up, my Heart, and Sing," whose position at the beginning of this work must have seemed odd to the more musically aware members of Bach's Leipzig congregation.[51] Rather than glorifying a newly built sanctuary [*Heiligthum*] with elaborate instrumental ritornellos and artful counterpoint, the latter version of this cantata begins simply, in four parts, with the more humble hut [*Hütte*] as a symbol for the heart; its focus is salvation. As Paul Gerhardt's hymn puts it:

Sprich Ja zu meinen Taten, Hilf selbst das Beste raten; Den Anfang, Mittl und Ende, Ach, Herr, zum besten wende!	Say yes to my deeds, lend your counsel for the best; Let beginning, middle and end turn out, oh Lord, for the best!
Mit Segen mich beschütte, Mein Herz sei deine Hütte, Dein Wort sei meine Speise, Bis ich gen Himmel reise!	Cover me with blessing, may my heart be your hut, Your word be my food, until I journey to Heaven!

The changed opening movement puts into a distinct context the recitatives and arias that follow: the various words that refer to buildings [*Haus, Tempel, Wohnung*] are now figurative rather than literal. For the 1726 performance it was no longer necessary to have a long duet recitative that questions entry into Heaven (no. 9), a bass recitative that refers specifically to a congregation and the building of a house (no. 10), nor an additional chorale (no. 6 of the 1723 version). Instead, this version ends with a duet on the joy of being chosen and "Pouring out your hearts here before God's throne and house!"

The recontextualizing of these movements is clarified by the addition of the obbligato organ, which first appears in the bass aria (no. 3).

50. The obbligato organ cantatas performed in Leipzig in 1726 include BWV 170, 35, 47, 169, 49, and perhaps 146. The reasons for Bach's repeated use of solo organ in the 1726 cantatas are not clear. The profound grief expressed in BWV 170 is perhaps related to the death, a month earlier, of Bach's three-year-old daughter, Christina Sophia Henrietta. She was his first child with Anna Magdalena Bach.

51. In addition to this work, extant Bach cantatas that open with a four-part chorale include only *Schau, lieber Gott, wie meine Feind* (BWV 153), *Ich lebe, mein Herze, zu deinem Ergötzen* (BWV 145), and *Ein' feste Burg ist unser Gott* (BWV 80b).

Was des Höchsten Glanz erfüllt,	What the radiance of the Highest fills
Wird in keine Nacht verhüllt.	will never be darkened by night.
Was des Höchsten heilges Wesen	What the Almighty's holy being
Sich zur Wohnung auserlesen,	has chosen for a dwelling-place
Wird in keine Nacht verhüllt,	will never be darkened by night,
Was des Höchsten Glanz erfüllt.	What the radiance of the Highest fills.

Divine light now infuses the human heart, no longer an earthly building, with the organ obbligato functioning as a kind of musical prism focusing this light on the faithful soul. The preceding recitative, which ends with the admonition that "this house be pleasing to You, may it be for Your countenance a true seat of grace, a light of joy," notes the necessary condition for salvation: a welcoming and believing spirit.

Further suggestions of a distinct message in the 1726 version of this cantata can be found in the nature of the obbligatos for organ, which are uncharacteristically simple. In the bass aria, for example, the right hand of the organ plays a musical line that is doubled by the first violin in all but three measures, leaving the organ as a soloist only from mm. 14 through 16, where there are four downward scales of five notes each.[52] The closing soprano and bass duet likewise includes a decidedly nonvirtuosic right-hand organ part whose consistent parallels with the first oboe leave it little room in which to maneuver.[53] With oboes virtually ubiquitous in Bach's Leipzig cantatas, the 1726 reassignment of the second oboe part in this duet seems an odd choice. And moreover, why was the single oboist who played in the final duet of this performance not given the original oboe part in the bass aria? The rescoring of both arias for obligato organ—which necessitated the copying of an entirely new part (see example 6)—seems especially strange when one considers that a violinist could also have covered the oboe part in the aria and the first oboe part in the duet by simply reading off the existing oboe part.

The overall effect of the changes made to *Höchsterwünschtes Freudenfest* in 1726, including its reordered sequence of movements, is a more personal message. In the 1723 version, the first-person singular is not mentioned until the second verse of the chorale that ends the first part; the previous movements employ the more neutral first-person plural. In the second part of the 1723 cantata, the singular pronoun occurs only in the final chorale; even the question of how one gets into Heaven (in the duet recitative) is posed in the third person, not the first. In the 1726 version, by contrast, the opening chorale sets a first-person context for the whole with a congregational-

52. The same part is assigned to oboe in the 1723 version, though it seems to have been played by two traversos in the largely lost Cöthen cantata (BWV 194a). On the likely instrumentation of BWV 194a, see the NBA I/35, KB, 143–51.

53. The same duet was originally accompanied by two oboes and continuo.

Ex. 6. J. S. Bach, *Höchsterwünschtes Freudenfest*, BWV 194/7 mm 1–17

style musical utterance. Even though the final duet remains in the first-person plural, its message is interpreted differently due to the preceding movements.

O wie wohl ist uns geschehn,	O how fortunate for us
Daß sich Gott ein Haus ersehn!	that God has found His house!
Schmeckt und sehet doch zugleich,	Taste and see that
Gott sei freundlich gegen euch.	God is well disposed toward you.
Schüttet eure Herzen aus	Shake out your hearts
Hier vor Gottes Thron und Haus!	here before God's throne and house!

In its new context, the duet's text is more oriented toward personal salvation than God's approval of a newly built or renovated church building. This very personal viewpoint, interestingly, is found in all of Bach's obbligato organ cantatas from 1726.[54]

This is not to say that a composer like Bach did not have deeper theological reasons for his use of obbligato organ; the present study has focused instead on associations that were common among German Lutherans in particular. Although in some cases the obbligato organ was a substitute for an unavailable instrument in a particular cantata performance, the vast majority of obbligato organ cantatas contain similar representa-

54. Note the use of the first-person singular in the obbligato organ cantatas already discussed, as well as in BWV 27, 35, 49, 71, 146, 169, 172, and 188.

tions of Heaven. This was particularly evident when the organ, the instrument that helps the congregation prepare for singing in Heaven, stepped out of its normal continuo role in the service's concerted vocal music and took on a special function. Like several of his contemporaries, Bach allowed his libretto to guide his instrumentation and frequently took advantage of the longstanding identification of the organ with Heaven. The instrument's multifacted associations with Heaven—in design, decoration, and placement; in dedication sermons, devotional materials, and cantata libretti—drew significant attention to its role in preparing the congregation for the afterlife, a theme surely dear to the heart of a committed church musician like Bach.

There is perhaps no better place to conclude this inquiry than with a poem titled "The Organ" written by the Bach admirer Friedrich Wilhelm Zachariae (1726–1777) and published in a large collection of his poetry in 1754. Zachariae was a student at the University of Leipzig during the mid 1740s, when he would have heard Bach's music and the Leipzig church organs on a regular basis.[55] His ode to the organ (reproduced in plate 4), the fourth poem in his first book of *Odes and Songs*, begins with sounds of the heavens—namely wind and thunder--before contemplating the last judgement and ascension into Heaven. It concludes by reminding us how the organ's sound forcefully draws us toward the music of Heaven and the choir of angels.

Do you hear the whooshing wind in the awaiting organ,
which prepares it for divine song?
Follow me, most worthy friend, down to the chilliest grave;
hallow yourself completely with pious music.

Heaven! Your jubilation rises up. The divine harmonious thunder
booming in our astounded ears.
The power of Heaven raises me up! Thus the halls of the temple
resound from the trumpets of this solemn day.

Under me the ground drones, and a lonely grave quakes,
greeted by the exhilarating sounds.
Thus, but still more powerfully, will the angel greet you,
with the holy trumpet of the last judgement.

55. Zachariae specifically mentions Bach in several of his writings: in a poem titled "Der Choral" that refers to the "singing of the sublime chorale with Bach's noble tones" (BDOK III, 660), in a tribute poem that refers to Bach and his melodic sons in connection to the greatest minds (BDOK III, 668), and in the preface to the second edition of the first volume of his collection *Scherzhafte Epische und Lyrische Gedichte*, where Zachariae notes that "the length of the arias [in *Die Pilgrime auf Golgatha*] is not pleasing to some critics of the arts and to composers, so I have made them shorter, although I am completely convinced that a long aria can be very well composed if you are a Bach or a Telemann" (Wilhelm Freidrich Zachariae, *Scherzhafte Epische und Lyrische Gedichte von Friedrich Wilhelm Zachariae: Neue durchgehends verbesserte Auflage. Erste Band*. (Braunschweig: Schröder, 1761) [I, 9].)

348 Oden und Lieder.

Die Orgel.

Hörst du den rauschenden Wind in der erwartenden Orgel,
Die er bereitet zum hohen Gesang?
Folge mir, werthester Freund, bis unter die schauernden Gräber;
Heilige ganz dich der frommen Musik.

Himmel! ihr Jubel hebt an. Die hohen harmonischen Donner
Brausen zu unserm erstaunenden Ohr.
Kraft von dem Hĩmel hebt mich! So klangen die Hallen des Tempels
Von den Trommeten des festlichen Tags.

Unter mir dröhnet der Grund, und einsame Gräber erzittern,
Von dem belebenden Schalle begrüßt.
So, aber mächtiger noch, wird sie der Engel begrüßen,
Mit der Posaune des letzten Gerichts.

Wenn

Erstes Buch. 349

Wenn nun der Richter erscheint auf der verblendenden Wolke,
Und in dem Felde der Todten es rauscht;
Wenn das belebte Gebein nun, seinem Erwecker gehorchend,
Stimmen der starken Posaune vernimmt.

Und dann der Richter der Welt die Heiligen um sich versammelt,
Oder Verworfne zum Feuer verstößt;
Und auf ihr Antlitz alsdann die Thronen und Cherubim fallen,
Vor dem Allmächtigen in Ehrfurcht gebeugt.

So geht der heilige Schall durch jubilirende Röhren,
Ungleich dem Schalle gemeiner Musik;
Reisset uns mächtig dahin zu Harmonien des Himmels,
Unter die Chöre der Engel verzückt.

An

Plate 4. F. W. Zachariae, "The Organ"

Now as the judge appears on the bedazzling clouds,
and whooshes through the fields of the dead;
Now as the resurrected bones, responding to their awakener,
hear the sounds of the strong holy trumpet.

And then the judge of the world gathers the holy around him,
or casts the corrupt into the fire;
and thereupon the throne angels and cherubim fall upon their face,
bent over in fearful reverence before the almighty one.

Thus the holy sound goes through jubilant pipes,
unlike the sounds of the common music,
forcefully drawing us there to the harmonies of Heaven,
enraptured among the choir of angels.[56]

56. Note that the two graphics published with the poem are not an organ, nor even organ pipes, but a bird singing in a tree and an angel resting on a cloud and blowing a trumpet.

Though Zachariae's poem may seem rather fanciful to us, it reflects how his world regarded the organ. Such sentiments, as we have seen, affected the design and decoration of the instruments themselves and what was said about them in hymnals, devotional books, organ dedication sermons, and especially in the texts of cantatas featuring obbligato organ. In the context of one of these works, the sound of the solo organ would "forcefully draw [listeners] to the harmonies of Heaven," whether the musical material from moment to moment offered energetic concerted lines, meandering arabesques, or just quiet solace.

CONTRIBUTORS

LYNN EDWARDS BUTLER is an organist and organologist with a special interest in the Baroque. She has played concerts on fine tracker organs in Canada, the United States, Europe, and Mexico, and is a Loft Recordings artist. In 1979 she co-founded and for the next twenty years directed the Westfield Center for Early Keyboard Studies. Author of numerous articles on the organ, she is currently writing a book-length study of organ builder Johann Scheibe of Leipzig. Her translation, *The Organs of J. S. Bach: A Handbook* (by Christoph Wolff and Markus Zepf), was published in 2012.

ROBIN A. LEAVER is emeritus professor of Sacred Music, Westminster Choir College, Princeton. He is currently visiting professor at the Institute of Sacred Music, Yale University, and honorary professor at Queen's University, Belfast, Northern Ireland. A past president of the American Bach Society, his most recent writings on Bach appear in *The Baroque Composers: Bach* (2011); *Exploring Bach's B-Minor Mass* (2013), the *Bach-Jahrbuch*, *Bach: The Journal of the Reimenschneider Bach Institute*. He is currently editing the forthcoming *Ashgate Research Companion to Johann Sebastian Bach*.

GEORGE B. STAUFFER is dean of the Mason Gross School of the Arts and distinguished professor of music history at Rutgers University. He is author of *Bach: The Mass in B Minor* (2003) and editor of *The World of Baroque Music* (2006). He is presently at work on the volume *Why Bach Matters*.

CHRISTOPH WOLFF is Adams University Research Professor at Harvard University, on the graduate faculty of the Juilliard School, and former president and director of the Bach Archive in Leipzig. He has published widely on the history of music from the fifteenth to the twentieth centuries, notably on Bach and Mozart. His numerous Bach publications include a seminal biography that has been translated into eight languages.

GREGORY BUTLER is emeritus professor of music at the School of Music, University of British Columbia in Vancouver, and past president of the American Bach Society. He is the author of *J. S. Bach's Clavier-Übung III: The Making of a Print* and numerous articles on the first editions of Bach's works. He has also written extensively on Bach's concertos, and a book-length study on the concerted works is presently nearing completion. He is collaborating with his wife, Lynn Edwards Butler, on a study of the Leipzig organs and organ works of Bach.

MATTHEW CRON earned a doctorate from Brandeis University, a master's degree from Smith College, and a bachelor's degree from the University of Massachusetts at

Amherst. He has taught at Boston University, Harvard University, and online at the Harvard Extension School and Rutgers University; he is currently on the faculty of the New England Conservatory of Music and Rutgers Arts Online. In addition, he is organist of Immanuel Lutheran Church in Amherst and on the board of directors of Multi-Arts of Amherst.

MATTHEW DIRST is professor of music at the Moores School of Music, University of Houston, and also serves as artistic director of the period-instrument group Ars Lyrica Houston. He pursues research and performance on organ, harpsichord, and as a conductor in more or less equal measure. A recent Grammy nominee, his recordings feature music of J. S. Bach, J. A. Hasse, and the Scarlatti and Couperin families; his publications include *Engaging Bach: The Keyboard Legacy from Marpurg to Mendelssohn* (2012).

GENERAL INDEX

INDEX OF BACH'S WORKS

KEYBOARD WORKS

INSTRUMENTAL WORKS

Bach Perspectives
is a publication of the
American Bach Society,
dedicated to promoting the
study and performance of the
music of Johann Sebastian Bach.
Membership information is available
at www.americanbachsociety.org.

The University of Illinois Press
is a founding member of the
Association of American University Presses.

Composed in 10/14 Janson Text
by Jim Proefrock
at the University of Illinois Press
Manufactured by Sheridan Books, Inc.

University of Illinois Press
1325 South Oak Street
Champaign, IL 61820-6903
www.press.uillinois.edu